FATHER

4

THE BRIDEZ

Erin —
Choose Love in
2019!
Steve

Stephen Kirr

*The journey of a father who used his
daughter's coming out to turn in.*

ISBN 978-1-64003-575-1 (Paperback)
ISBN 978-1-64003-576-8 (Digital)

Covenant Books, Inc.
11661 Hwy 707
Murrells Inlet, SC 29576
www.covenantbooks.com

"Dedication"

Ladies, your love and courage throughout this journey has inspired me to pursue the life I have always imagined.

Jaclyn and Jordy
Honeymoon, Ireland

The Journey

Sometime in your life you will go on a journey.
It will be the longest journey you have ever taken.
It is the journey to find yourself.

—Katherine Sharp Quotes, Quotables, quotabl.es

Father 4 the Bridez, wedding day

To thine own self be true,
And it must follow, as the night the day,
Thou canst not then be false to any man.

—William Shakespeare
(Hamlet Act 1, scene 3, 78–82, enotes.com, Inc.)

CONTENTS

ACKNOWLEDGMENTS

The number of people that have provided me with encouragement, assistance, and support over the past three plus years during the writing, editing, and publishing process is numerous.

However, it is imperative that I take a brief moment now to thank certain individuals and express my sincere gratitude for their belief, love, guidance, and assistance to help make this dream a reality.

First and foremost, I must give all the praise and glory to my Source, Creator and Living God; the words that fill these pages flow from him through me.

To our bridez, Jordy and Jaclyn, thank you for loving each other and providing me the opportunity to love you. I also want to sincerely thank you both for allowing me to share your story so together we can help others to choose love.

To my bride of thirty-four-plus years, Lori, thank you for sharing me nightly with the computer and always believing in me even when I doubted myself. In the words of Tom Cruise as sports agent Jerry Maguire, "You complete me." It is through your constant belief in me that this book is a reality.

To my son, Adam, who has shown me the power of living creatively and in the moment with love.

To our loving cousin Susan Sysler for volunteering weeks of her life to edit an uber mess, your extremely kind remarks concerning the book gave me the impetus to persist.

To the multitude of sages and teachers that have so greatly influenced my soul, Dr. Wayne Dyer, Mother Theresa, the Dalai Lama, Lao Tzu, Ram Dass, Ramana Maharshi, Kahalil Gibran, Paramahansa Yogananda, Sister Catherine Ann, all the sisters at Saint Rita, along with all the friars at Archbishop Curley.

To my attorney, accountant, publisher and marketing company, for without your skills and expertise, this book would only exist on my Dell.

Thank you All!

INTRODUCTION

Thank you for choosing Father 4 the Bridez!

I am truly grateful!

This book was written for you.

I have been extremely blessed in my life and it is my hope that you will be able to take away a few ideas you can use to positively change your life or the life of someone else.

Friends and family have asked me "why" I titled the book, "Father 4 the Bridez." Allow me to explain, I am Jordy's father, and have a deep love for Jaclyn my daughter in law. There are 4 core universal beliefs identified in our relationship with source. (chapter 6) Our Brides are magnificent and deserve a unique spelling hence the "Z."

Objectives

- ❖ Share the story of my daughter Jordy's coming out, love affair and marriage to her wife, Jaclyn.

- ❖ Document milestone events and legal advancements that contributed to greater equality for the LGBTQ (lesbian, gay, bisexual, transgender, and questioning) community from 1960 to modern day.

- ❖ Reveal my lifelong struggle for spiritual growth and enlightenment

- ❖ Offer you a few simple takeaways and tools to help you live the life you have always imagined.

Outcomes

- ❖ Embrace the four universal *core beliefs* as a pathway to spiritual enlightenment.
- ❖ Understand that the door to spiritual growth always opens inward.
- ❖ Make the journey from embarrassment to embracement (if necessary).
- ❖ Choose **LOVE**

Namaste,

Father 4 the Bridez

THE NEWS

*Nothing travels faster than the speed of light
with the possible exception of bad news,
which obeys its own special laws.*

—Douglas Adams
("The Hitchhiker's Guide to the
Galaxy," quotations page.com)

For Philadelphia in winter, it was relatively mild, the average daytime temperature fluctuated between thirty-three to thirty-seven degrees with intermittent sun and a light wind blowing at about five to seven miles per hour. It was Wednesday, February 23, 2011, and I will never forget the day, the time, and where I was when I received the call that would forever change the course of my life.

The day was typical for me at this time, working as a brand manager for a national commercial bakery. I traveled extensively from New York to Virginia ensuring that the quality of our products coupled with passionate service fueled the growth of the business that remains healthy and expanding to this very day.

When I was on the road, as I was this day away from my family and home in Baltimore, it was common for me to log twelve- to fourteen-hour days. The morning began with a workout at 5:00 a.m. in the closet-like gym at the Marriott Courtyard. As road warriors can attest that if more than two people arrive at the same time, the space filled with a treadmill in dire need of a tune-up, a broken rowing machine and a rubber mat, it gets crowded quickly. Luckily for me, I was able to sail through my workout without incident and was prepared to greet the day with eternal optimism.

Being that it was February, it got dark early, and the workday ended as it had begun. Albeit long, it was fruitful. The hotel was undergoing renovations at the time, and the normal counter for check-in was now a folding table in a room adjacent to the plastic-covered entryway.

15

The change in venue for the hotel staff led to a monstrous bottleneck, which was exacerbated by an uncooperative guest who acted as if he was checking into the Plaza hotel in New York, complete with special instructions for specific room amenities, all for the grand price of $119 per night.

After quickly checking into my room, I made a beeline for the Plymouth Meeting Mall to grab dinner to enjoy while watching TV and writing up my day's report for submission to the home office before heading off to bed.

The mall was unusually crowded for the middle of the week at 7:00 p.m., but I was able to commandeer a Greek salad with chicken to help satisfy my rapidly growing appetite. I was tired, cold, and hungry and just wanted to eat, finish my work, and go to bed. Then it happened. My cell phone rang.

Caller ID revealed that it was my wife, Lori, my bride of twenty-six years. I was convinced that this would be our routine evening call, nothing unusual. "How was your day?" Followed by a brief but always comforting good-night chat.

The instant I heard my wife's voice, I could immediately tell that something was not right. Normally, Lori's voice was booming and cheerful, but tonight it was dripping with uncertainty and apprehension.

It quickly became clear she had some news to share with me that caused her to reflect this tonality. After several minutes of small talk, the conversation came to an abrupt end, followed by silence, a sigh, and . . .

My daughter Jordy was twenty-one years old and in her senior year at Georgetown University. We were very proud of Jordy's athletic and academic accomplishments, and we looked forward with great anticipation to her final season on the women's lacrosse team and graduation in May.

This was a time of great enthusiasm and excitement for our family, and we were eager and prepared to partake in all the graduation festivities that Old Hilltop[1] had to offer.

---

[1]	Term of endearment for Georgetown University, Washington, D.C., depicting the original 60 acres of land procured in 1789 by Bishop John Carroll on a hilltop overlooking the village of Georgetown.

In the fall of the previous year, Jordy was selected to be one of the captains for the women's lacrosse team for the upcoming spring season. Jordy had more than earned the privilege to be hailed as one of the leaders for her senior season as she played an integral role in the success of the Hoyas in three previous campaigns.

It was preseason, and my wife had made the one-hour drive to Georgetown, located in a bucolic section of Washington, DC, perched on a hill overlooking the Potomac River; she was there to watch the team play an exhibition game against the English national team that was in country on tour.

On this day, like many others in the previous three years, my wife arranged to enjoy a postgame bite to eat with Jordy. They chose one of their favorites, the Tombs, the iconic Georgetown ratskeller built in a Federal-style town house in the heart of Georgetown, with history dating back to the mid-1800s. It was to be a time to catch up on the team, school, impending graduation, and potential job opportunities.

As I awaited Lori's next words with quiet anticipation, they suddenly burst over the line.

"Our daughter is gay."

During their dinner, Jordy informed my wife that she was gay and that she had come out to her coaches and the team earlier that week.

The words "Our daughter is gay" hung on the line for what felt like an hour, when in reality only several seconds had passed.

My wife was waiting. How would I react? What would I say?

Patiently Lori stood by in desolate silence, allowing me the opportunity to process the news, graciously giving me the time and space that I am sure she would have treasured just hours before as she dealt with the life-altering news face to face.

Finally, Lori roused me from my thought coma with a very soft and reflective, "Well, what do you think?"

Think? What do I think?

Luckily for me, I had spent the past several months immersed in audio books by Dr. Wayne W. Dyer. I remember my exact words with an aura that felt like an outer body experience.

I softly, calmly, and fearlessly echoed words that I had heard just days and weeks before but did not fully comprehend their meaning until that very moment;

"Honey, our children come through us, not from us. It is our job to love her through this."

My words were the words of Dr. Dyer, yet I truly embraced them. The words became real for myself and my wife, and at once the tension on the line subsided.

I knew at that very moment the storm had passed, and by jointly committing to love our daughter through what had to be a very difficult time, we would forever preserve our relationship with her and with one another.

The balance of our conversation that evening was filled with inquisitive banter. How did she arrive at this place in her life? How long has she been gay? Did we somehow have an effect on this decision? Was this a choice, or was it innate? Does she have someone in her life?

Come to find out, none of these questions were broached during my wife's dinner with our daughter, out of shock, fear, or simply naïveté. We had a lot of questions, little or no answers, but we did have what we both needed the most. We had each other's commitment to love her unconditionally and to faithfully ensure that our daughter would always have the opportunity to pursue happiness and to live the life she was destined to fulfill.

As we ended the conversation, Lori asked me to please give Jordy a call and to let her know just how much we both loved and supported her, just as she had done in person hours before at the restaurant. It was clear Jordy was awaiting my call and my response.

I would have only one chance to convince her that we had nothing but love in our hearts and that she had our unwavering support, just as she always had enjoyed throughout her life.

The call to Jordy was emotionally charged, overflowing with my countless use of the words *love* and *support*. She was genuinely relieved to know that both Mom and Dad were squarely in her corner prepared to help her through life now as an openly gay person.

Jordy also took the opportunity with both my wife and now me to reinforce her desire to have children and a family. I guess this was the extended olive branch that would serve to satisfy the traditionalist in us.

Little did I know that my journey had just begun. I sat on the bed blankly staring at my dinner that had gone untouched over the course of what was now an hour. Exhaustion overcame me. I had no desire to eat, write a report, watch television, or do anything at all. For the first time I could ever remember, I had no ability to function. I just wanted to sleep.

I awoke from my restless slumber at 4:00 a.m. trying to recall the events from the evening before. Surely it was a dream. Most certainly what I thought was real did not occur. I tried to sit up in bed, but my heart and head were both throbbing as if having consumed a bottle of cheap whiskey the night before.

Normally a quick riser and a devoted morning person, I was sluggish and had no desire to complete the day's appointments that lay ahead. I resembled a boxer that had been hit with multiple head shots. I was dazed and confused. What was wrong with me? From what I could recall from the evening before, I had handled the news well with both my wife and my daughter, but something was wrong with me. Something was terribly and inexplicably wrong.

The next several weeks were strangely uncomfortable. When I was at home with my wife, we actually avoided discussing the news as well in the presence of other family and friends not in the know. However, I felt this insatiable desire to share the revelation but did not. I must admit, my wife was much more comfortable with my daughter's sexual orientation than I was, and she began sharing the news almost immediately with select family and friends without my knowledge.

I want to be clear, I loved my daughter (still do) and had the desire to wholeheartedly support her decision to live the life she was predestined to live, but my parochial and traditional upbringing and life experiences were not making it easy. I am a product of eight years of Catholic elementary and middle school followed by four years of high school under the auspices of Franciscan friars. These feelings of conflict were not going away at the snap of a finger.

My religious and cultural upbringing were raging a war in my mind and soul. I was trapped between fundamental Catholicism coupled with a hearty dose of blue-collar, lower-socioeconomic mentality versus the person I aspired to become. A person filled with love, acceptance, humbleness, humility, and compassion consistently connected to my source.

I was a mess. I knew the path that I wanted to traverse, yet this inner tug-of-war was making it next to impossible for me to consistently move forward. Every time I thought I had turned the corner, the EGO would make its way to the surface and squelch my progress.

Dr. Dyer was the first teacher to introduce me to the acronym of EGO, which can be interpreted by some as Edging God Out. This simply implies that when we are disconnected from source, our carnal way of thinking and acting take over. When this occurs, it normally spells trouble, confusion, frustration, and often self-flagellation.

Outwardly I was saying and doing all the appropriate things that were in alignment with source but in direct conflict with the noise in my head.

I was caught between two worlds, my old ways of thinking and acting and my desire to be a person of excellence, one that thought and acted in a consciously connected manner.

I knew I needed to understand myself better than I did. Can you imagine awakening at fifty-one years old and realizing you do not even know who you are, what you want to be, or where you want to go?

That in a nutshell was my problem. For the better part of my life, I equated my value as a person by where I grew up, where I went to school, what I did for a living, what kind of car I drove, what kind of vacations we took, where we sent our kids to school, and when I was going to be wealthy enough to retire. Maybe I never came out and said these things publicly, but this was the turmoil that embroiled my thinking day in and day out for the better part of my adult years.

Now I had a daughter who was gay.

I should have been rejoicing that she had not attempted to harm herself or elect to commit suicide along the way as she carried the heavy burden of this earthly proclaimed disease.

I should have been celebrating her courage to come forth after so many years of keeping this a secret. This is a secret that many never have the ability to reveal for fear of public ridicule or, worse yet, disdain and disconnect.

I shamefully recall a conversation that I had with parents of one of Jordy's classmates from the McDonogh School.[2]

In 2001, my daughter, Jordy, was twelve years old and had been at the school since the second grade (now in the sixth grade). We had been out with this family several times before, and our daughters were beginning to become very good friends. You could say that we were all becoming very comfortable with the choice of topics and the depth of the conversations.

Generally, we would go out as families, our friends bringing their other children while we would bring my son Adam (fifteen at the time of this conversation). However, we had determined that our friendship had grown to the point where the four of us would dine without the comfort of the children being the bane of our evening conversation.

We settled on a little restaurant in the heart of old Greektown on the fringes of downtown Baltimore by the name of Zorba's Bar & Grill. Anthony Quinn (who played Zorba in the famous movie *Zorba the Greek*) would have been delighted by the decor and the quality of the food. Authentic Greek dishes, such as *dalmades* (grape leaves) and lamb chops, led the menu as favorites, while the nautical accessories complete with the fisherman net and sea creatures complete the ambiance.

We were operating in unchartered waters with our friends, once again without the safety net of the kids. It was Saturday night, time to let the hair down and enjoy the island in time called the weekend. During dinner, we all enjoyed a cocktail and shared a bottle of wine.

---

[2]   McDonogh School is a private coeducational institution in Owings Mills, Maryland.

Somehow, the conversation landed on the question, what would you do if you found out that you had a gay son or daughter?

Our friends answered first, they were (and most likely still are) very cerebral and liberal in their thinking, reflecting their expensive educations, Jewish heritage, and New York City life experiences. As you can guess, not to stereotype, they espoused thoughts, feelings, and opinions dripping with empathy, compassion, love, and support. Our friends offered the very same thoughts, feelings, and opinions that I enjoy today. The same way one would think and feel if they were fully connected to source.

I can honestly say that I have lived a life of very few regrets or shame, but this might be my weakest and most vulnerable remark I ever uttered. Not sure where it came from, this faceless EGO rose up and declared, "I would disown my son or daughter for choosing this lifestyle."

I still recall the looks on their faces. They both looked at me with sheer disgust and shock. In an attempt to allow me the opportunity to rethink the comment and possibly save face, the father asked me a different question, "So you mean to tell me that if Jordy came home tomorrow and told you that she was gay, you would disown her?"

I now realized the gravity of my hubris, ignorance, and disconnect with my source and softly said no.

The pain and personal embarrassment that I experienced by this horrific revelation of ignorance just into my fourth decade (forty-one) on earth led me to deeply explore my inner being and reignite my sojourn for self-discovery.

THE 60'S

*If someone thinks that peace and love are just a
cliché that must have been left behind in the 60's
that's a problem. Peace and love are eternal.*

—John Lennon
English Singer, Songwriter and Political activist,
member of the "Beatles, (1940-1980)

I arrived into this world on Thursday, June 30, 1960. The president of the United States was Dwight D. Eisenhower, the most popular song on the radio was "Everybody's Somebody's Fool" by Connie Francis, and Alfred Hitchcock had just directed the movie *Psycho* starring Anthony Perkins, Janet Leigh, and Vera Miles.

The Pittsburgh Pirates (MLB), Boston Celtics (NBA), Philadelphia Eagles (NFL), Ohio State University (college football), and Floyd Patterson (boxing) were all champions in their respective sports.

I am the son and youngest child of William "Bill" Kirr and Helen Travagline (maiden name) Kirr.

My sister Renee was already two years my senior and had blazed a path for my arrival. My father's life was fairly typical of a lower-middle-class male at this time in our country's history. A high school graduate, a veteran with a four-year stint in the Air Force (during the Korean War), married young, had a couple of kids, and went to work in a steel mill (Bethlehem Steel) for the remainder of his adult life.

My mother traversed a similar path: high school followed by a brief stint in the secretarial pool at Bethlehem Steel, married young, had two kids, and spent the rest of her adult life as a stay-at-home mom.

Together in 1957, they bought a red brick row house, named accordingly as all the homes were connected in a row and grouped together in clusters of six, for $9,800 along with a 30-year 3 percent mortgage.

The house had three stories along with three bedrooms, one full bath, a small kitchen, dining room, living room, and a finished knotty pine club cellar.

A slim fenced-in backyard just large enough for a Weber grill, a cooler of Natty Boh (brewed in Baltimore), and a picnic table for the summer cookouts completed our property.

We were living the American dream (so we thought). Dad had a secure factory job, Mom was content staying at home raising the kids, and for the time being, the United States was not at war.

Eastfield (my hometown) was adjacent and situated to the northeast of Dundalk, Maryland. Dundalk is south and east of the city of Baltimore, at the time a thriving port. Church Road (our street) was aptly named as there was a church on the corner adjacent to the McDonald's, the fastest-growing food franchise in the country.

Eastfield-Dundalk was the home of the blue-collar factory worker in Baltimore in the sixties. At the time, Bethlehem Steel Corporation at Sparrows Point employed more than thirty-thousand men and women. The area also enjoyed a plethora of blue collar factory jobs fueled by the likes of General Motors, Lever Brothers, Westinghouse, and Crown Cork and Seal.

The chamber of commerce had a bumper sticker plastered on every automobile in the area "Live, Work, Shop Dundalk." The men went into the factories, the women to the secretarial pool or stayed at home to raise the children. This was a scene right out of a Norman Rockwell painting.

We (Eastfield-Dundalk) were a group of people who worked hard, drank hard, were passionate about our local sports teams, the Orioles and Colts, and believed that this was the end of the rainbow.

However, this was not the gay rights rainbow. This was the blue-collar pot of gold that life had to offer. This was it, and that was just fine.

About ten doors down from our house lived two lesbians. One was the daughter of our next-door neighbor Ms. Marie and her husband. Our next-door neighbors were two hardworking and very nice people.

Ms. Marie and my mother were good friends and would often go shopping together on a Saturday afternoon at Schocket's, a discount department store in the Polish section of Baltimore City, named Highlandtown.

Our neighbor's daughter was always very respectful of my mother and father and treated my sister and myself in a similar fashion. However, her partner was a hard-charging, motorcycle enthusiast who enjoyed running with a group involved in nefarious activity.

In hindsight, this was probably not the best place for them to be living in the 1960s. Our street, our neighborhood, our town was filled with ultraconservative straight families with children. Their flamboyant lifestyle challenged the status quo and provided a poor example of gay women, which forever was embedded into my mind. This couple's way of life did little to stem the growing tide of dislike for gay and lesbians in our neighborhood.

Then it happened. One night, a disgruntled friend, enemy, or drug dealer blasted a hole in their front door with a shotgun, and our quiet little street was never the same. These two lesbians had brought violence and horror into our neighborhood and reinforced every negative connotation known to man about the gay lifestyle. So at a very young age, I was challenged and developed a negative impression of lesbians and their way of life.

As a result of this incident, my best friend's family, who just happened to live next door to the lesbian couple, promptly put their house up for sale and moved across town.

Our lives were forever affected by this occurrence brought about by these two gay women who, we thought, were clearly not as morally righteous as we. (Remember this was the Sixties.)

Looking back on what happened, I am sure that what transpired was not nearly as traumatic as I remember it to be at the time. I harbor no ill will toward either of the young ladies and their families; however, I was dealt a very powerful mental blow at an early age, one that would take me years of education and spiritual exploration to overcome.

Growing up in my neighborhood in the sixties was seemingly just fine, as we had no idea of just how poor we really were. Thank God, and we did every Sunday at our local Catholic parish, Saint Rita.

Our house was situated directly behind a public elementary school that my sister and I did not attend. It also was adjacent to a strip of land that was along with knee-high weeds and high tension towers and wires. Day in and day out, we played every sport known to mankind in the shadows of these buzzing electrical towers and wires.

Little did we know of the harmful effects that resulted from years of exposure to these towers. As if the exposure to the electrical towers and wires was not bad enough, we awoke each day to red soot covering our cars, lawns, and outdoor furniture.

This fine red soot was the by-product of the steel-making process at Bethlehem Steel, which was just a few miles away. This emission was a combination of coke and iron generated from the blast furnace that was an integral part of the steel making process at Sparrows Point.

Welcome to Eastfield-Dundalk in the 1960s. Personally the Sixties were a time of growth and fun. I went from the womb to the middle of fourth grade in 1969.

It was during this period that I discovered and fueled my love of sports. I played organized soccer than football in the fall, basketball in the winter, and at the time, baseball in the spring. When I was not practicing or playing for my community teams, I was playing the sport of the season in the neighborhood with one or more of the other kids on my street.

Unlike most neighborhoods today, mine was filled with kids looking to play just about any time of day. I was able to walk out my back door and have a pickup football game with six to nine kids per side, a basketball game down at the school courts five versus five, or a rubber ball baseball game with my best friend Mike in no time flat. I played sports nonstop. The only other activities that I did on a regular basis during this period was eat, sleep, go to school, do homework, and go to church.

On November 22, 1963, our young and inspirational president, John F. Kennedy, was assassinated by a massively depressed and misaligned former Marine sharpshooter by the name of Lee Harvey Oswald in Dallas, Texas. Every person old enough to understand what occurred on this day knows exactly where they were when they heard the horrific news.

Vice President Lyndon Baines Johnson took the oath of office on the tarmac at Love Field in Dallas shortly after President Kennedy was declared dead. A small coterie of staff and Mrs. Kennedy looked on in complete shock and awe of the day's events, while the lifeless body of John Kennedy lay in a coffin in the rear of Air Force One.

Upon taking office, President Johnson worked tirelessly enacting social programs that aided the less fortunate, giving them a "hand up, not a handout."

Several of these social programs still exist today, such as Medicare and Medicaid, which assist elderly and low-income citizens pay for health care. Another of these programs was Head Start, which prepared young children for school, and a Job Corps that trained unskilled workers for jobs in the postindustrial job market.

However, as the war in Vietnam was heating up, the war on poverty became too expensive to properly fund. Soon after Johnson took office, he escalated the commitment to the war effort. In 1964, Congress authorized President Johnson to take "all necessary measures" to protect American soldiers and their allies from the communist Viet Cong, and within a few days the military draft was enacted.

The draft personally touched our family as my mother's youngest brother was drafted into the army and sent to Vietnam to serve our country.

During the Sixties, I do remember nightly watching on our one black-and-white twenty-inch television set the daily casualty report from Vietnam. In between regular-scheduled programming, a clip from the day's combat would be shown with the number of killed and wounded for the day and the totals since the war's inception.

I recall going on several trips to visit my uncle when he was stationed stateside, but it was upon his return that we would experience the Vietnam War up close. The time served in the war zone changed my uncle from a fun, loving, and carefree athlete into a troubled veteran. The man that returned home was challenged by multiple addictions, rage, and moral infidelity.

This was a scenario taking place all over the country, and the fabric of our society was being torn apart by war, drugs, sexual exploration, and the beginning of the end of the traditional family unit.

My father worked shift work at the steel mill. He would rotate his work hours almost every week unless of course he was able to make a trade with another guy in his department that had the same job.

One shift was called midnight. This is when you begin your shift at 11:00 p.m. and work until 7:00 a.m. One working this shift arrives home at about 8:00 a.m., unless you stop at the local watering hole on the way home.

This shift causes you to have to sleep during the daytime, which was very difficult for my father to do. Hence this sleepless week caused the rest of the family to be on notice.

The next shift, identified as daylight, was my father's favorite. He would arrive at work around 6:00 a.m. and work until about 2:00 p.m. This shift was perfect for a multiple-hour stop at the local shot and beer joint on the way home and still be on time for dinner, which was historically served between 4:00 to 4:30 p.m., when my sister and I were in elementary and middle school.

The infamous third shift was aptly labeled three to eleven, the exact time he was expected to be at work. Often the boys from the mill would decide to blow off some steam until the wee hours of the morning, returning them to their homes and bed between 2:00 to 3:00 a.m. This shift was better than midnight but still left the burden of sleep to the daytime hours.

The life of a steelworker's wife was hard and lonely. She was left to take care of almost all the children's responsibilities, not to mention all the cooking, cleaning, shopping, and carpooling (if there were two cars in the family).

My mother was the glue that held our family together. On a typical day she would rouse us from sleep, feed us, dress us, make our lunches, drive us to school, and then return home to take care of the house.

Mom would also go grocery shopping with my father if he was home and do it all by 3:00 p.m., when we needed to be picked up from school.

Then it was time to prepare dinner; help us with our homework; get us off to football, basketball, baseball, or softball practice (my sister); do the dishes; and clean up the kitchen. At which time we returned home only to need a snack, get a bath or shower, and get us tucked in to bed.

My mother took great pride in her domestic duties, and I can hardly remember a time when I heard her complain about her lot in life. It was a simple life, but one I believe she found very rewarding.

Our future success was her validation of a life lived with great purpose. She only wanted us to have a better life than she, and for this I am eternally grateful.

By the late 1960s, gay and lesbian subcultures and communities had grown in many of the nation's cities, complete with bars, cabarets, magazines, and restaurants.

> The counter culture movement was in full swing in the 60's. One quote that is often used to identify this time period is, "Turn on, Tune in, and Drop out" made popular by Timothy Leary, a noted Harvard lecturer and advocate of LSD. Leary spoke to more than 30,000 hippies at Golden Gate Park in San Francisco in 1967 and uttered the famous phrase which lends itself to the LSD experience, peace and many other issues prevalent at this time. Figuratively, Turn on, meant to go within to activate your senses. Tune in meant to interact harmoniously with the world around you and Drop out suggested an active, selective, graceful process of detachment from one's commitments, also interrupted to mean self-reliance, mobility, choice and change. Timothy Leary, American psychologist and author (1920-1996)

I did not have helicopter parents. Not only did they not hover over me, but they were nowhere to be found.

I never minded the fact that they did not come to my practices or games. It was normal back then in my neighborhood. Parents had to work or were busy taking care of other siblings or simply trying to grab a moment for themselves.

Fourth of July truly was the single holiday that best evoked small town life in the Sixties. The day began with the entire town of Dundalk turning out for the local parade that snaked its way around miles and miles of residential homes, parks, the town square, and small businesses closed for a day of celebration.

The parade was the morning's focus of attention, complete with police cars, fire trucks, local politicians waving from their convertibles, beauty queens, local sports heroes, and of course, marching bands.

According to tradition, metal and plastic chairs were strategically placed along the parade route as early as the night before to garner the best views.

Adults sat in chairs, as the children lined the parade route sitting on the cement curb, eager to hear the fire engines and the marching bands.

In the 1960s, Dundalk was the largest unincorporated community in the state of Maryland. An unincorporated area is a region of land that is not governed by its own local municipal corporation, but rather is administered as part of a larger body, such as a county. The town was given its name after the town of Dundalk, Ireland.

> *Dundalk from the Irish, Dun Dealgan meaning "Dalgan's stronghold," and is the county town of County Louth, Ireland. It is located on the Castletown River which flows into Dundalk Bay and is close to the border with Northern Ireland, equidistant from Dublin and Belfast.* (National register of historical places, Dundalk historic district)

Once the parade was over, we all rushed back to our houses for an afternoon cookout (not a barbecue).

This feast was complete with hot dogs, hamburgers, potato salad, macaroni salad mixed with small canned shrimp, and Schmidt's Blue

Ribbon Rolls washed down with Shasta cola for the kids and Pabst Blue Ribbon or National Bohemian (Natty Boh) beer for the adults.

The day was filled with family, food, fun, friends, and fireworks that lit up the sky right behind my house.

January 12, 1969, began with such great anticipation and excitement as my football heroes, the Baltimore Colts, were taking on the New York Jets in Super Bowl III.

The game was purely a chance for the mighty Colts from the old and established National Football League (NFL) to take on the newcomers from the upstart American Football League (AFL) in front of a national audience at the Orange Bowl in Miami, Florida.

The Colts were superior in every statistical metric and entered the Super Bowl by crushing a formidable opponent the Cleveland Browns by the score of 34–0.

The Jets backed into the game, returning a lateral that was thought to be blown dead for a game winning score and a 27–23 win over the Oakland Raiders.

The Jets entered the game an 18-point game time underdog, and it appeared this would be no match for this highly skilled veteran Colt squad. The Colts were led on offense by arguably the best backup quarterback that ever played the game in Earl Morrall.

Earl started most of the season, replacing the great John Unitas, who was hampered by a chronic sore elbow.

The Jets, on the other hand, had a very exciting and brash four-year veteran quarterback out of Alabama named Joseph William ("Joe Willie") Namath, also known as "Broadway Joe."

Being nine years old and intensely passionate about the Colts, the day turned into one of my very worst as a Baltimore sports fan as Joe Namath led the Jets to a stunning 16–7 victory.

I never thought I could experience such complete and utter devastation until later that year when the New York Mets would beat the Baltimore Orioles in the World Series and the Knicks would beat the Baltimore Bullets for the championship of professional basketball.

One of the greatest feats of the 1960s occurred on July 20, 1969, as Apollo 11 landed the first human beings, astronauts Neil Armstrong and Buzz Aldrin, on the moon.

Armstrong became the very first to step onto the lunar surface six hours later on July 21 at 2:56 UTC. Armstrong spent about two and a half hours outside the spacecraft. Aldrin slightly less, and together they collected 47.5 pounds of lunar material for return to earth.

The third member of the trip was Michael Collins, who is credited with piloting the command spacecraft alone in lunar orbit until Armstrong and Aldrin returned to it just under a day later for the trip back home.

So as the decade of the Sixties came to a close, it was clear this was a new world. The staid and conservative ways of the forties and fifties had come to a screeching halt in the halcyon days of a decade marked by radical personal growth and exploration.

Personally the core foundational building blocks of my life had been laid. The family unit was mother, father, brother, sister, grandparents, aunts, uncles, and cousins.

A man and a woman were meant and designed to be together, to get married, to have children, and to live happily ever after.

The man was the breadwinner in the household, while the woman was to take care of the children and the home.

Extended family was natural, and all Sundays and holidays were a time when family was to gather, to overeat, overdrink, oversmoke, argue incessantly, watch sports, and complain about having to go to work on Monday.

The 60's

LGBTQ Milestones

> During the 1960's reformers within the legal profession argued in favor of decriminalizing private, consensual adult homosexual relations, on the grounds that government should not regulate private morality.

> (Timeline: Milestones in the American Gay Rights Movement, PBS.org)

> On January 1, 1962, Illinois repealed its sodomy laws, becoming the first state to decriminalize homosexuality.

> (Timeline: Milestones in the American Gay Rights Movement, PBS.org)

> In 1963, the Supreme court ruled that a magazine featuring photographs of nude males was not obscene and therefore not subject to censorship.

> (Zeitlin v Arnebergh, Docket No. LA 26905)

> On July 4, 1965, at Independence Hall in Philadelphia, picketers begin staging the first Reminder Day to call public attention to the lack of civil rights for LGBT people. The gatherings continued for five more years.

> (Timeline: Milestones in the American Gay Rights Movement, PBS.org)

> On April 21, 1966, members of the Mattachine Society stage a "sip-in" at the Julius Bar in Greenwich Village, where the New York Liquor Authority prohibits serving gay patrons in bars on the basis that homosexuals are disorderly. Society

president Dick Leitsch and other members announce their homosexuality and are immediately refused service.

Following the sip-in, the Mattachine Society will sue the New York Liquor Authority. Although no laws are overturned, the New York City Commissioner on Human Rights declares that homosexuals have the right to be served.

(Timeline: Milestones in the American
Gay Rights Movement, PBS.org)

➤ In August 1966, transgender customers become raucous in a 24 hour San Francisco cafeteria, management calls the police. When a police officer manhandles one of the patrons, she throws coffee in his face and a riot ensues, eventually spilling out into the street, destroying police and public property.

(Timeline: Milestones in the American
Gay Rights Movement, PBS.org)

➤ On June 28, 1969, New York City police raided the Stonewall Inn, a Greenwich Village bar whose patrons included transvestites, gay men and lesbians. Raids of gay and lesbian bars were commonplace at this time. Instead of yielding to the police the patrons fought back, three days of unrest followed the incident. This incident ushered in a new era for gays and lesbians in the United States: an era of pride, openness and activism. It led many gay and lesbians to "come out of the closet" and publicly assert their sexual identity and to organize politically. In Stonewall's wake, activist organizations like the Gay Liberation Front transformed sexual orientation into a political issue, attacking customs and laws that defined homosexuality as a sin, a crime or mental illness. (History. com, Gay Bars: A place of refuge: Stonewall Inn)

THE KISS

What the world needs now is love sweet love.

—Jackie DeShannon, 1965
Jackie DeShannon, American singer–songwriter,
"What the World Needs Now", 1965

It was midmorning on Sunday January 5, 2014, and the Green Bay Packers were preparing for their NFC wild card matchup with the San Francisco 49ers. Throughout the day, weathermen across the country were making claims that the game time temperatures would dip below freezing by kickoff with wind chills reaching as low as -25 degrees.

Three years ealier, Jordy graduated from Georgetown with a degree in English and a minor in theology. She was fortunate enough to use her Hoya connections to secure a position with SB Nation[3].

Jordy thrived as a young advertising support manager challenged daily to ensure that the clients, national household name brands, enjoyed every opportunity for success with their online marketing campaigns.

Pinning for the opportunity to remain connected with the sport of lacrosse, Jordy was invited to join the staff of the St. Stephen's & St. Agnes School[4] for the spring 2012 season.

The school enjoyed a rich history of success in women's lacrosse. Jordy enjoyed her experience as a high school coach, and little did she know how well the experience would serve her in just a few short years.

In the summer of 2012, an opportunity arose for Jordy to help open a new SB Nation office in Chicago. Always with a flair for

---

[3] In 2011, the fastest-growing online sports media brand and the largest network of fan-centric sports communities, and a division of VOX media, in the heart of DC.

[4] St. Stephen's & St. St Agnes School is "an independent Episcopal coed private college prep school in Alexandria, VA.

the adventurous, she contacted an old college teammate living in Chicago and made arrangements for the two of them and another friend to share some space downtown.

Once again Jordy quenched her desire to coach women's lacrosse by joining the staff at the Loyola Academy. The Loyola Academy[5], like St. Stephen's & St. Agnes, was a perennial powerhouse program. Jordy was excited to serve the high school program as a varsity assistant during the spring season and an Under Armour All-American coach during the summer.

As it would be, this ad hoc volunteer coaching opportunity would pave the way for Jordy to be considered for an NCAA Division I (D1) coaching opportunity at Marquette University[6] in the upcoming fall.

The view was beautiful from Jordy's eleventh-floor studio apartment overlooking Lake Michigan. Jordy was now living in Milwaukee, Wisconsin, and working as the assistant women's lacrosse coach at Marquette University

Like Georgetown, Marquette enjoys a world-class reputation for excellence academically and athletically.

Jordy was preparing for her inaugural season as a division one lacrosse coach and was excited to get the 2014 season underway. She had arrived on campus in June 2013 and immediately went to work, hitting the ground running as she scurried to and from a myriad of recruiting tournaments throughout the summer.

Working under the tutelage of a young and very talented head coach, Jordy was learning what it was like to now coach at the collegiate level.

The Marquette women's lacrosse program was in its second full season as a division one program, making the transition from a club sport.

---

[5]   The Loyola Academy "is a private co-educational college prep school in Wilmette, IL, a northern suburb of Chicago.
[6]   Marquette is a private, coeducational Jesuit university located in the heart of downtown Milwaukee, Wisconsin.

The coach, a collegiate All-American, was an experienced assistant coach for multiple D1 programs and the perfect mentor for Jordy and the young team.

The 2013 season ended with just one victory, but the team added a very talented freshman class, and the excitement from the fall campaign gave birth to the anticipation for the start of the spring season, which was now just weeks away from beginning.

Frantically Jordy searched for layer upon layer of clothing and accessories to wear to the game. Even though it was only 10:00 a.m., she could tell that by the time the game stated at 3:30 p.m., it was going to be bitterly cold and windy.

A good friend had secured a quantity of tickets for the game, primarily driven by the below frigid forecast coupled with the NFL's decision to lift the television blackout.

> *Fox 6 along with a group of Packers corporate sponsors purchased the remaining available tickets on Friday January 3rd to ensure a sellout and TV broadcast of the game though out Wisconsin.* (Fox6now.com, January 3, 2014, Fox 6 Milwaukee, Local TV LLC)

Even with the news of the game being available in the warmth and comfort of her apartment, a friend's house, or one of Milwaukee's many bars and restaurants, Jordy was going to the game.

> *The National Football league television blackout policies are among the strictest of the four major sports leagues in the country. Since 1973, the NFL has maintained a blackout policy that states that a home game cannot be televised in the team's local market if all the tickets are not sold out 72 hours in advance of its start time.* National Football League television blackout policies (1973-2014)

The car was loaded with four friends and enough food and adult beverages to get them through a week on a deserted island. The 120-mile trip took a little over two hours and landed the crew at the frozen tundra of Lambeau Field three and one half hours prior to game time.

They would have ample time to partake fully in the sacred ritual of pregame tailgating. However, due to the ungodly weather conditions, the friends would utilize a heated tent structure on the grounds outside of the stadium.

As she has been fond of doing since her college days, Jordy bought her group a round of shots to get the blood flowing.

To her surprise, she was informed that each shot was only four dollars, a mere pittance compared to the prices back on M. Street in Georgetown. The news sparked a bevy of purchasing that would continue right up until game time.

Just days prior to the playoff game, Jaclyn Simpson, the assistant women's volleyball coach at Marquette, was introduced to Jordy through a mutual friend in the athletic department. As fate would have it, they would both receive tickets to make the trip together to Green Bay.

A native of Downers Grove, Illinois, and an All-American volleyball player at the University of Wisconsin, Jaclyn was no stranger to cold weather. Jaclyn's coaching journey included a stop at the University of Iowa under her mentor and one of the brightest young coaches in all of women's volleyball.

As fate would have it, Jaclyn is the physical opposite of Jordy, statuesque at just over six feet tall and supported perfectly by an athletic frame that complements her long hair and attractive facial features.

Three years Jordy's senior, she was mature and worldly beyond her years primarily due to her opportunity to play professionally in both Germany and Cyprus.

Prior to Marquette, Jaclyn spent two seasons as the assistant women's volleyball coach at East Carolina University. It was here that Jaclyn completed her graduate degree earning a master's in sports psychology.

As the day progressed, the weather continued its winter dance, offering bitter cold, wind gusts, snow showers, and intermittent sun dominated by heavy grey clouds that kept the fans bundled tight and using one another's body heat to ward off the extreme elements.

Welcome to Green Bay Packer weather in January, not something the likes of which Jordy had ever experienced.

Green and gold filled the party tent, the parking lot, and the streets that dominated the entire Lambeau stadium landscape. Only on rare occasion did you spot the rust and gold that adorned the San Francisco 49er fan.

Oddly enough, the Packers began the 2013 season on the road versus the very same 49ers. The Packers would lose the game in the fourth quarter by the score of 34–28 despite a terrific performance by packer great Aaron Rodgers.

In week 9, the packers lost at home to their fierce rivals the monsters of the midway the Chicago Bears. In this game a sack by Shea McClellin on a third and eight on the Packers' first possession of the game caused Rodgers to suffer an injury that would prevent his return.

Taking advantage of the Green Bay misfortune, the Bears held Packer backup QB Seneca Wallace to 11/19 for 114 yards and 1 interception for a 27–20 win.

Week 10 proved to be even more of a challenge without starting QB Aaron Rodgers as the Philadelphia Eagles came into the friendly confines of Lambeau Field and defeated the pack 27–13.

This time it was Green Bay QB Scott Tolzien trying to fill the cavernous void left by the all pro. The result was the same, another loss dropping the Pack to 5–4 on the season.

In front of 79,114 at MetLife Stadium, East Rutherford, New Jersey, the New York football Giants dismantled the now-withering Pack in a week 11 matchup 27–13.

Now 5–5 on the 2013 campaign, the Packers were on the ropes and looking forward to heading back to Lambeau for a conference matchup with the Vikings.

Trailing 23–7 at the start of the fourth quarter, Packer QB Matt Flynn led the pack to a 26–26 tie and a 5-5-1 record after 11 games. If the Pack were going to make the playoffs, they would need to perform well over the balance of the final 5 regular season games.

They did enough, as the Packers would manage to win three of their last five games, ending their season with an 8-7-1 regular season record, edging out the Chicago Bears, who finished the season 8-8, for the NFC division title and the right to a wild card matchup with the 49ers.

As the afternoon turned to evening, the skies darkened, and the snow showers rained down on the Packer faithful, now making their way into Lambeau for the impending kickoff.

Today's matchup was being carried by the Fox network, and the great team of Troy Aikman and Joe Buck would be announcing the game. Sideline and feature reports would come from both Pam Oliver and Erin Andrews, in many opinions the best team in television.

The game time temperature was a balmy 5 degrees, mostly cloudy with a wind chill of -10. Despite the weather conditions, 77,525 braved the elements to cheer on their hometown team. This was the Packers, the playoffs and an opportunity to continue to advance to the biggest game in professional sports, the Super Bowl.

In the meantime, the crew had settled into their seats and was enjoying a bird's-eye view of the pregame festivities from their corner end zone perch.

In no time flat, they made friends with all the surrounding Packer faithful adorned in cheese heads and doing their very best to ignore the elements.

Jaclyn and Jordy were slowly but surely becoming more comfortable with each other as the day progressed. Engrossed in the new relationship, the two young women were starting to let go and enjoy each other's company. Something very real and exciting was happening: they were falling in love.

Due to the weather, playoff nerves, and whatever else we can blame it on, the first quarter ended with just two San Francisco field goals by kicker Phil Dawson (22 and 25 yards). The first quarter respite left time for a brief visit to the restroom and a refill on the beers. Surely the Pack would be ready to play come quarter number 2.

The second quarter offered much of the same, a defensive struggle, as the two teams scrambled to find their offensive prowess. Finally with 5:56 to go in the quarter, Aaron Rodgers found Jordy Nelson for a five-yard touchdown, the pack took the lead 7–6.

The joy was short-lived as the 49ers responded just several minutes later as running back Frank Gore found pay dirt with a ten-yard touchdown scamper to put the 49ers back on top 13–7.

The Pack was able to manage one final drive that stalled inside the 49ers' twenty-five yard line and settled for a Mason Crosby field goal with just four seconds left on the clock.

At halftime, the 49ers led the Packers, 13-10.

The two-hour drive from Milwaukee plus the three and half hours of pregame partying coupled with the seventy-minute-plus first half in the extreme cold of the Wisconsin night spelled signs of fatigue for the revelers from Marquette.

However, this was not to be the case as the friends used one another and the electricity of NFL playoff football game to sustain them until the start of the second half, one they knew that would be filled with excitement and ultimately a ticket to the next round of the playoffs.

Ed Hochuli, the NFL's premier referee, signaled the start of the second half, and the crowd became energized and wildly displayed their optimistic enthusiasm that this would be the quarter that the packers would take charge of the game.

To everyone's dismay in the stadium and watching on television, the third quarter ended as it had begun, with the 49ers clinging to a 13–10 margin. Both defenses were playing outstanding football with the all-pro 49er linebacker Navarro Bowman leading all defensive players in tackles, ending the game in double digits with 10 solos.

Fueled by the excitement of the growing relationship, the two star-crossed lovers began to become increasingly intimate as they invented ways to hold and caress each other throughout the third quarter of play. As the others began to recede into the rhythmic cadence of the game, Jordy and Jaclyn were just beginning to hit their stride.

As the fourth quarter began, the meat locker-like conditions were clearly taking their toll on players, fans, officials, and everyone involved in making this game a reality. However, offensively it started well for the Packers as they moved the ball down the field and punched in a one-yard touchdown run by John Kuhn and just like that the Packers were out in front 17–13, and the Packer faithful came to life.

In the corner of the end zone, the couple bathed in the excitement of the Packers' touchdown, igniting a spark of passion emanating from their daylong embrace moving the couple to the next natural phase.

Jordy was now standing on her seat while Jaclyn stood on the stadium floor. In unison, the two pulled back their wool face masks, pushed up their glasses, and brushed back their hair to join their lips for the first time as a couple, to be known in perpetuity as The Kiss.

No sooner had Jordy and Jaclyn unlocked their lips and embraced, the 49ers had once again regained the lead on a twenty-eight-yard touchdown pass from Colin Kaepernick to tight end Vernon Davis to make the score 20–17.

It was no longer bitterly cold. It no longer even mattered that the Packers were losing. The only thing that mattered was that two soul mates had found each other. It was Fourth of July in January as the sparks fanned flames of love.

Once again the Packers would answer the call. This time it was a Mason Crosby's twenty-four-yard field goal that would tie the game with only 5:09 remaining in regulation. Could the Packers stop the resurgent 49er offense one more time, get the ball back, and still have time for a drive of their own?

The game would come down to one big play, with time running out, facing a fierce blitz on a third and eight. Kaepernick eluded the Green Bay defenders to scramble for eleven yards that set up the eventual game-winning yard field goal by Phil Dawson as time expired.

In the seventh coldest game played at Lambeau Field since 1959, and the fourth coldest postseason game in Packer history, the 49ers would prevail 23–20 and advance to play the Carolina Panthers.

The 49ers would continue their winning ways the following week and go on to beat Carolina setting up an NFC Championship clash with the Seattle Seahawks, in a contest that ultimately sent the Seahawks to Super Bowl XLVIII and a crushing victory over the Denver Broncos 43–8.

The warmth of the car's heater was incredibly inviting as the cold, windswept crew began peeling off layer after layer of coats, sweaters, hats, scarfs, and gloves in an effort to arrive at some level of comfort for the two-hour ride home.

This was the end of a very long and adventurous day. It was now time to head south on Highway 43, destination, Milwaukee.

As everyone settled in, Jordy and Jaclyn used this opportunity to continue The Kiss they began inside Lambeau field.

The only ones left awake were the girls and the driver; the others were sound asleep, the natural result of the travel, the elements, the alcohol, and the disappointing season-ending loss.

By the time Jordy settled into her bed on Prospect Avenue, it was almost midnight, but the excitement of the day continued to pump her with adrenalin that would keep her awake for a few more hours, trying to understand the gravity of what had taken place in the span of less than twenty-four hours.

Jordy was not looking for a relationship; she had been through a tumultuous affair back in Chicago that did not end very well. She had arrived at Marquette to earn her graduate degree in sports management and leadership, which she ultimately completed in two years while coaching full-time with the hope of gaining valuable experience as an assistant at the division one level.

Staring out over Lake Michigan, from the warmth of her one-room apartment high up in the Wisconsin sky, Jordy smiled. She knew that this day was special, that Jaclyn was special, and the kiss at Lambeau would live in her heart and mind forever.

> *You kissed me! My head drooped low on your breast With a feeling of shelter and infinite rest, While the holy emotions my tongue dared not speak, Flashed up as in flame, from my heart to my cheek; Your arms held me fast; oh! Your arms were so bold—Heart beat against heart in their passionate fold. Your glances seemed drawing my soul through mine eyes, as the sun draws the mist from the sea to the skies. Your lips clung to mine till I prayed in my bliss they might never unclasp from the rapturous kiss.* ("You Kissed Me," Josephine Slocum Hunt)

THE 70'S

In the seventies we had to make it acceptable for
people to accept girls and women as athletes.

—Billie Jean King (Professional tennis player,
Advocate for gender equality and social justice,
equalplayforequalplaytennis.wordpress.com)

On September 20, 1973 women's tennis star Billie Jean
King faced off against 55 year old former Wimbledon
Champion Bobby Riggs, dubbed the Battle of the Sexes.
Riggs hyped the event saying, "The best way to han-
dle women is to keep them pregnant and barefoot." In
front of more than 30,000 spectators at the Houston
Astrodome and millions more watching on television,
including yours truly, King dominated Riggs in three
straight sets. The confluence of sports and sexuality had
come to a head, as the openly gay King shocked the male
dominated sports world with her victory. King's victory
coupled with the passage of Title IX, an anti-gender dis-
crimination law is often credited with sparking a boom
in women's sports. (September 20, 1973, King Defeats
Riggs in Battle of the Sexes)

The seventies ushered gay and lesbian rights into our living rooms
via television and newspapers. The sixties had blown the lid off of the
discussion, but the seventies was the decade of marked mainstream
success.

In 1970 the gay and lesbian movement did not exist in my universe. My world was dominated by sports and my beloved Baltimore
Colts. On January 17, 1971, just two years after the colts lost to
the New York Jets in the super bowl they were back at the Orange
Bowl in Miami, this time taking on the Dallas Cowboys a formidable opponent from the now National Football Conference (NFC).
During the merger and reorganization of the two separate leagues,

now there was one league but two conferences. In the shuffle, the Colts went from being a part of the old guard NFL to the new American Football Conference (AFC).

This time the roles were reversed for the Colt quarterbacks as Unitas played most of the game and Earl Morrall came on late to lead the Colts to victory. The game was a defensive struggle as both quarterbacks would throw two interceptions in the game. However, the play of the game was a multitipped ball that settled into the hands of Hall of Fame tight-end John Mackey, who would rumble forty-five yards for a touchdown to cap off a seventy-five-yard play.

The game was ultimately to be determined in the last five seconds of the contest as rookie kicker Jim O'Brien would seal the Super Bowl victory with a thirty-two-yard field goal! My elation was at an all-time high. My Colts had avenged their loss from two years ago, and now I could proudly proclaim that we were the champions of the football world.

Finally the sports world was once again coming into focus as just several months before in October the Baltimore Orioles defeated the Cincinnati Reds to win the 1970 World Series.

Even though I was short, I loved to play basketball, and as a highly impressionable basketball fan during the 1970s, the Baltimore Bullets would play the Milwaukee Bucks in the 1971 championship, which they would lose to the great Lew Alcindor (a.k.a. Kareem Abdul Jabbar) and the Big O, Oscar Robertson, four games to zero.

Later in the decade, the now Washington Bullets would take on Rick Berry and the Golden State Warriors in 1975, also losing in four straight games.

Finally our championship would be claimed as the 1978 Washington Bullets led by the Big E, Elvin Hayes, and Wes Unseld outlasted the Seattle Supersonics in seven games. The Bullets would once again return to the NBA finals in 1979, this time giving way to the Seattle Supersonics in five games.

The seventies offered me the opportunity to attend and experience three educational institutions that were very influential in shaping who I am today.

Saint Rita

Saint Rita elementary and middle school (1970–1974) was the place where I learned how to be a Christian, develop good study habits, and play lacrosse for the first time.

Saint Rita is situated squarely in the center of the town of Dundalk, and the teachers were primarily sisters from the order of Immaculate Heart of Mary with a smattering of lay teachers. My favorite teacher was very young, kind, and sweet-natured person we fondly addressed as Sister Catherine Ann.

Sister Catherine Ann demonstrated a unique combination of patience, compassion, teaching skills, and toughness with love.

I have always fondly remembered her passion for literature and the desire to make us the very best students we had the ability to become. At a time when dominance or threats were a commonplace methodology among the order, Sister Catherine Ann would blaze her own path with love and kindness.

Saint Rita parish and school was the heart and soul of Dundalk in the seventies. It was the home of the families that predominately spent their working lives in the many factories nearby.

The sons and daughters of these families were tough-minded, intelligent, and for the most part, very interested in getting a good education and pursuing the American dream.

Looking back now, I am filled with great pride in my fellow classmates at Saint Rita school. We became a very accomplished class, complete with military leaders, doctors, attorneys, politicians, business leaders, and clergy.

The history of St. Rita Church is one of creation and steward-ship. In 1922, Archbishop Curley decreed that a new church be built to administer to a group of about two hundred overflow parishioners of St. Luke Church in Sparrows Point who met for weekly mass in the Community Hall, Dundalk Building, on Shipping Place.

Fr. Joseph Weidenhan, the first pastor of St. Rita, was instructed to build a rectory and continue holding services in the Community Hall. But plans soon changed; he was to build a church as well because the Community Hall was being made into apartments.

Providentially, at that time Bethlehem Steel agreed to donate one acre to any church that would build a permanent structure within a year. As St. Rita Church had no land, Fr. Weidenhan was quick to accept the challenge and bought an additional acre from the company.

The parishioners cleared the trees, and in November 1922, a small wooden structure with a short bell tower was erected where the parking lot is today. A rectory was built on the corner of Dunleer and Dunmanway in 1923.

By February 1926 enough money was raised by the parish to clear more of the two-acre plot to build an eight-room school and a convent.

The cornerstone was laid on May 26, 1926, and on September 6 of that same year, five sisters from the Sisters, Servants of the Immaculate Heart of Mary, Scranton, Pennsylvania, welcomed 126 students at a cost of $1 per month per student.

Over the next twenty years, the school and church both flourished. By 1943, the parish was totally free of debt. In 1947, St. Rita parish celebrated its silver anniversary with a mass in Heritage Park. Soon, however, it became clear that debt would again have to be incurred due to the success of both church and school. A cornerstone for the new church to replace the temporary wooden structure was laid on December 4, 1949, and what is now the current church was built near the old one.

Fr. William Migliorini began his stewardship of St. Rita Parish in 1975. He instituted devotion to St. Francis of Assisi and observed St. Rita's feast day, which the parish would celebrate in May for the next ten years. The parish enjoyed financial stability under his leadership.

Archbishop Curley , HS

Archbishop Curley High School (1974–1978) is the place where I became a man.

Archbishop Curley is an all-boys Catholic high school, located in Baltimore, Maryland, in a tough part of the city at the corner of Sinclair lane and Erdman Avenue. The staff at Curley during my time was composed of 70 percent Franciscan friars from the order of Saint Francis and the balance being lay staff.

The school is dedicated to Archbishop Michael J. Curley (1879–1947), who served as the tenth archbishop of Baltimore from 1921 to 1947.

It was the first Archdiocesan high school in Baltimore established for the education of young men. The school is accredited by the Maryland State Department of Education and the Middle States Association of Colleges and Schools.

Archbishop Curley High School opened its doors in September 1961 to a pioneer class of 420 freshmen. It was formally dedicated on April 17, 1962, by Lawrence Cardinal Sheehan, the successor of the late Archbishop Keough.

In December of 1969, after extensive renovation, the Lawrence Cardinal Sheehan Library and Multi-Media Instructional Center was dedicated. It was the first building in the Archdiocese of Baltimore to be dedicated to His Eminence, Cardinal Sheehan (1898–1984), who had been a long-time friend and supporter of Curley.

The area where Curley was located historically was home to a melting pot of immigrant blue-collar families, primarily people of Polish, Irish, and Italian descent.

In the seventies, the neighborhood began to change as these hardworking families evolved and moved out into the suburbs. As the demographic began to change, so did the landscape.

Eventually the entire surrounding neighborhood changed, making attending Archbishop Curley High School challenging and oftentimes dangerous.

However, as the area around Curley became tougher, inside the chain-link fence, the school was flourishing.

Curley, like Saint Rita, had a similar makeup of those that would attend during this time frame. We were the sons of lower- to middle-class families, all wanting the same thing for their children: an opportunity to succeed.

I loved Curley, and I embraced every aspect of the culture.

It would be here that I would excel academically, athletically (football and lacrosse), socially, and spiritually.

Academically I would ultimately graduate number 17 of 216 in my class. I enjoyed all subjects except foreign language (French) and passionately pursued English, religion, and history.

The friars at Curley were truly remarkable as teachers and builders of men. It was here in these classrooms that I learned how to formulate my own opinions, collaborate with classmates, and become a leader.

The friars modeled their lives and their humble way after Saint Francis of Assisi. Saint Francis was an Italian friar and preacher, founder of the Order of Friars Minor and the women's Order of Saint Claire. Saint Francis is most often associated with his vow of poverty, love of nature, gentleness to animals, and humility toward his fellow man.

Each morning in homeroom, we would recite the following:

The Prayer of Saint Francis

Lord, make me an instrument of your peace,
Where there is hatred, let me sow love;
where there is injury, pardon;
where there is doubt, faith;
where there is despair, hope;
where there is darkness, light;
where there is sadness, joy;
O Divine Master, grant that I may not so
much seek to be consoled as to console;
to be understood as to understand;
to be loved as to love.
For it is in giving that we receive;
it is in pardoning that we are pardoned;
and it is in dying that we are born to
eternal life. (Saint Francis of Assisi)

Athletically, I enjoyed great success at Curley. I was very fortunate to play with some very gifted and skilled athletes while benefitting from passionate and caring coaches.

Entering my freshman year, the sport I loved playing the most was baseball. I would never have the opportunity to play at Curley. The baseball program was one of the best in the area and featured one of the top professional pitching prospects at this time, my classmate Tim Norris. Tim would be drafted in the fourth round, the hundredth player chosen in the 1978 major league baseball draft by his hometown, Baltimore Orioles. Tim played five years in the minor leagues winning the Southern League title for the Charlotte Orioles (AA) in 1980 with his friend and teammate Cal Ripken Jr.

There comes a time when young athletes who enjoy playing multiple sports in the same season have to make a choice. I was fortunate; the Curley baseball coaching staff made my decision an easy one. Lacrosse, like baseball, is played during the spring; it was time to get serious about lacrosse.

Curley was just starting to produce winning lacrosse programs when I arrived on the scene in 1974. The Friars had won championships in 1969 and 1971 respectively. During my tenure, we won back-to-back championships in 1976 and 1977.

Lacrosse gave me the best chance to succeed in sports, and it would prove to be my gateway to a full and rich life. Little did I know that this game with the crazy stick and rules would come to be a lifelong obsession. Spiritually, I was a sponge. My time at Saint Rita had prepared me well for the challenge, and I was eager to take my faith to greater heights. I enjoyed every aspect of my Curley religious experience.

Curley in the mid- to late Seventies was a magical place. The school was growing, the young men that attended the school were from good, hardworking families, and the friars and lay staff were dedicated to our success.

In 1978, I was voted Ideal Curley High Man of the Year. This is an award presented annually to the graduating senior who is deemed by the staff to have excelled in all areas of student life.

I was a member of the National Honor Society, varsity lacrosse and football team, and the Black Friars theater club.

By the time I graduated, I was given a chance to play lacrosse at the highest collegiate level at the United States Military Academy at West Point.

First, though, I would be required to attend the United States Military Academy Preparatory School due to my low (by West Point standards) SAT and ACT test scores.

In order for me to gain entrance into West Point, I would first have to spend one year at the United States Military Academy Preparatory School at Fort Monmouth, New Jersey.

Part of the West Point preparatory school experience (circa 1978) was the military mandate that each student be an active member in the United States Army. Hence, in order to become an enlisted man, one first has to graduate from basic training.

So at the ripe old age of eighteen and a newly minted high school diploma, I arrived at Fort Dix, New Jersey, to begin my eight weeks of basic combat army training.

Fort Dix in 1978 was beginning to show the decline of the US military fighting force. The Vietnam War had ended three years prior, and the country was still reeling from the fifty-eight thousand United States servicemen killed in action.

The United Sates would end up being embroiled in the conflict in the jungles of Southeast Asia for over twenty years.

America as a country was tired of war, and the idea of being in the military at this period in time was not very appealing to many young men and women graduating from high school.

My time at Fort Dix went quickly. I was now a lean, mean fighting machine, with a whole new list of skills to add to my résumé, including but not limited to being a marksman, skilled in the use of an M16 rifle, M60 machine gun, and light anti-armor weapon (LAAW).

Physically I was in the best shape of my life, or so I thought. We ran over one hundred miles during our training, which did not include time spent on countless trips to the obstacle course, force marches, or the grenade range.

United States Military Academy Preparatory School (USMAPS)

In 1978, West Point prep was housed in the concrete olive drab buildings on the grounds of Fort Monmouth. Located in central New Jersey, Monmouth was just a brief drive to the beaches of Long Branch and Asbury Park

If you have ever listened to FM radio, received a speeding ticket, or wondered what life was like on other planets in the galaxy, you have had an impact by the work done at New Jersey's Fort Monmouth.

The work done at the sprawling base near the Jersey shore led to communications advances, including the development of the afore-mentioned FM radio, radar, and the ability to bounce signals off the moon. By the time the Unites States entered the war in Afghanistan, the folks at Fort Monmouth had developed the phraselator, a system that translated the English voice into Dari, Pashto, Arabic, and other languages.

Life at prep school was challenging but fun. During the week, we were soldiers who performed like any other active duty personnel, but the weekends were for the most part free. Once we completed our classroom obligations on Friday afternoon at about 4:00 p.m., we were off until 6:00 p.m. Sunday evening.

Many weekends were spent either making the two-and-one-half-hour drive back to Baltimore to see friends and family or in a hotel room by the Jersey shore with several buddies from the class.

For those of you too young to remember, 1978 was the height of the disco craze in America. The music scene was raging with a mix of heavy metal, ballad, and disco all taking their segment of the marketplace. Several years before in 1975, Bruce Springsteen, a native New Jersey son, born in Freehold, burst onto the music world with his best-selling album *Born to Run*, with lyrics that resonated with the average person struggling to make a life in America.

Like many young people at this time, I was trying to understand who I was and what I wanted to do with my life. Was I a soldier who wanted to commit to a military life and career, or was I the son of lower-socioeconomic parents who desperately needed the military to fund my college education?

In 1970, singer-songwriter Alice Cooper released the hit single "I'm Eighteen." The song accurately depicted how I felt as an eighteen year old in 1978. I'm a boy and I'm a man, I'm Eighteen and I like it.

The year at Fort Monmouth passed quickly. I was fortunate to be surrounded by so many wonderful young men and women who encouraged me every step of the way to follow my dream of gaining entrance into West Point.

All my hard work would bear fruit as I was able to raise my college entrance scores to meet the West Point standards.

West Point

Upon graduation, I entered the United States Military Academy at West Point, New York, in the summer of 1979. During my plebe year (first year cadet), I enjoyed success on the lacrosse field, making the varsity team and having the privilege of being coached by Richard "Dick" Edell, a wonderful man and Hall of Fame coach.

The banks of the Hudson (Hudson River) produced a cornucopia of great military leaders throughout history, including but not limited to Robert E. Lee, Ulysses S. Grant, Dwight Eisenhower, George Patton, and many more too numerous to mention. The long gray line is formidable. I am proud to have gained entrance and attended the academy.

I completed my academic plebe year, with a solid C- average and enough demerits to choke the army mule. After multiple conversations with numerous academy staff, it was determined that it would be best for me to take my talents to College Park, Maryland.

To give you a better idea of what I am talking about, my French professor agreed to have mercy on me by giving me a C-if I promised never to step foot into France, an agreement I happily made and kept until well into my forties.

Militarily, I was no General Patton. As a card-carrying member of I Company, Fourth Regiment, we gained our reputation by our motto, quit the corps, and join I4.

We were the last of the last, last billets near the old gym, last in parades, and last in military acumen.

I generated my fair share of demerits and did the minimum to pass inspections and muster daily.

My teammates, coaches, and classmates were fantastic, many I still call friends today, some thirty-seven years later.

It was time to change the set of my sail.

The 70's

LGBTQ Milestones

> On June 28, 1970 celebrating the first anniversary of the Stonewall Rebellion, the first U.S. lesbian and gay pride march took place. The organizer Fred Sargeant, leading the group climbed the base of a light pole and was astonished to see that thousands had joined the march, there was no fanfare what so ever, no floats, no music, no boys in briefs as the police turned their back on the scene in disdain, but the masses of people kept carrying signs and banners and chanting and waving at the onlookers that now lined the street to garner a glimpse of this amazing happening. (Fred Sargent, 1970: A first person account of the first gay pride march, villagevoice.com)

> 1972. An ABC made-for-TV movie "That Certain Summer" featured Hal Holbrook and Martin Sheen as a gay couple. That is believed to be the first same-sex couple in a TV program. In the same year, the United Church of Christ became the first U.S. mainline/liberal church to ordain an openly gay man. He was William Johnson founder of the LGBT coalition. ("That Certain Summer" ABC, November 1, 1972, The Paley center for media, paleycenter.org)

> 1973. Kathy Kozachenko became the first openly gay candidate to run for office in the United States. She was elected to the city council of Ann Arbor, Michigan. (Kathy Kozachenko, Activist, Politician, Biography, lgbthistorymonth.com)

> 1974 witnessed many landmarks in the struggle for gay and lesbian rights as the American Law Institute updated its Model Penal Code, a group of laws that they suggest be implemented at the state level. They recommend to legislators: "private sexual behavior between consenting

adults should be removed from the list of crimes and legalized." The American Bar Association expressed its approval. The membership of the American Psychiatric Association voted to remove homosexuality from its list of mental illnesses: the Diagnostic and Statistical Manual of Mental Disorders (DSM). The first International Gay Rights Conference was held in Edinburgh, Scotland. (American Law Institute, (ali.org), American Bar Association, (americanbar.org) & American Psychiatric Association, (psychiatry.org))

➢ 1975 marked the Vatican's opinion that homosexual orientation (feelings) was not wrong, because one's orientation is not a matter of choice; it is something that is not chosen. However, they stated that to act upon one's feelings by engaging in a homosexual act is a sin, whether it is in a casual or in a committed relationship. (Vatican.va)

➢ 1976. The National Conference of Catholic Bishops (in the US) stated that "homosexuals . . . should not suffer prejudice against their basic human rights. They have the right to respect, friendship and justice." (United States Conference of Catholic Bishops, usccb.org)

➢ In 1977, Anita Bryant, runner-up in the 1958 Miss America contest, a Southern Baptist, and spokesperson for the Florida Citrus Commission became incensed by a gay rights ordinance in Dade County, FL and launched a successful campaign for its repeal in June of that year. This triggered a spontaneous march by gays, lesbians and their supporters in San Francisco—the first of many. "She ripped open the closet door that society had held shut for centuries. She put the 'gay' issue on the front pages of every newspaper," Webmaster Uncle Donald commented. (PBS.org)

➢ On November 8, 1977 the openly gay Harvey Milk won a seat on the San Francisco Board of Supervisors and becomes responsible for introducing gay rights ordinance protecting gays and lesbians from being fired from their jobs. Milk also leads a successful campaign against proposition 6 an initiative that forbids homosexuals from teaching.

On November 27, 1978 Harvey Milk was assassinated at City Hall in San Francisco. That evening, a candlelight march was held from the Castro District to City Hall. The march became an annual event. (Harvey Milk, American Politician (1930-1978), New York Times, nytimes.com)

➢ In 1979 the second gay riot in the U.S. occurred when the murderer of Harvey Milk received a light jail sentence. It became known as the "White Night Riot." (The San Francisco "White Night Riots" of 1979 by Bruce Martinez, libcom.org)

Jordy Kirr, Georgetown Lacrosse   *William & Helen Kirr*

Bethlehem Steel, Sparrows Point, Maryland

Renee Kirr   *Stephen Kirr*

Main Street, Dundalk, 1960 (dundalkhistory.org)

Dundalk Fourth of July parade route

Jordy and Jaclyn, Packers Game

*Jordy, assistant coach,
Marquette lacrosse*

Packers v. 49'ers, Jordy and Jaclyn's Corner View

Stephen Kirr, Saint Rita

Saint Rita Church, November 1922

Michael J. Curley (1879–1947)

Archbishop Curley High School

Senior prom, 1978

Basic Training,
FT. Dix, NJ (1978)

USMA Prep School,
1978-1979

USMA, 1979-1980

BUTCH'S RESTAURANT

A restaurant is a fantasy—a kind of a fantasy in which diners are the most important part of the cast."

—Warner LeRoy[7]
(Warner Leroy (1935-2001), Restaurant Impresario,
quotation 1976, New York Times article, 2.24.01 by Eric Asimov)

Situated at the southwest corner of W. Michigan and N. James Lovell Streets in Milwaukee, Wisconsin, was Butch's Old Casino Steak House. The owner was a serial restaurateur by the name of Butch Schettle.

Before the arrival of Carson's, Morton's, Capital Grill, Ruth Chris, and Rodizio Grill, the Brazilian steak house, there was Butch's. In its day, Butch's was the place for business leaders, athletes, and politicians to enjoy a cocktail, angus steak, cigar, and lively banter with the owner, bartender, and waitresses.

Butch's was an old-time restaurant decorated with vintage slot machines and other eclectic antiques, but by 2014, it had seen its better days, and soon thereafter the restaurant closed its doors after the final service on March 28, 2015.

Butch's building had become very valuable since it became the home for the restaurant in 1994 (which was first opened in 1986 at the corner of N. Water and Pleasant Streets) and was the final piece of the land puzzle that was necessary to make way for the construction of the Marquette University Milwaukee Bucks sports medicine and athletic center.[8]

Jordy was in the midst of her inaugural spring season as the assistant lacrosse coach at Marquette. Jordy had met Jackie several months before and were clearly falling in love. To the best of my

---

[7]   Warner LeRoy (1935-2001), Restaurant Impresario, owned Tavern on the Green and the Russian Tea Room.

[8]   Ultimately the deal would fall through and Marquette would elect to build their athletic facility in a different location

recollection, my wife, Lori, had met Jaclyn, but this would be my first meeting, and Butch's was to serve as our backdrop for our first get-together as a family.

I remember the night like it was yesterday. We were to begin the evening's festivities by meeting at Jordy's apartment, which was just ten floors above the room we were staying. The apartment complex had a guest room on the first floor across from the exercise room and down the hallway from the main entrance and lobby.

I recall being a bit nervous, perhaps more curious than anything, as we dressed and prepared to meet the girls. As we ascended the elevator to Jordy's eleventh-floor studio apartment, it occurred to me that this just might be the person my daughter would choose to spend the rest of her life with as a gay couple.

We knocked lightly on the door and let ourselves into the apartment. The girls were in the kitchen, which is a miracle in itself due to its miniature dimensions. My wife and I actually passed the girls and would position ourselves to meet inside the main room near the round table used this evening as a buffet for a variety of appetizers.

Jaclyn exited first, and I was completely taken back by her imposing but stunning presence. She radiated Midwestern wholesomeness and carried her athletic frame of six feet with grace. Even today some three-plus years later, I am in awe of her natural beauty and grace.

From the very first moment forward, I loved everything about Jaclyn. It was easy to see how my daughter could quickly be drawn in to her easygoing manner coupled with her passion and drive to be the very best in her profession.

Loving Jaclyn was going to be easy. Getting used to being with them both in public would be a different challenge that I would have to overcome.

Jordy went out of her way to make our pre-dinner gathering a success. Every detail was addressed. A cornucopia of fresh appetizers were paired with wonderful wines accompanied by fresh flowers and candles.

The ladies were fashionably dressed and ready to share their love with us. Our cocktail hour quickly passed with everyone enjoying the opportunity to get to know one another a tiny bit more.

It was a typical early spring Milwaukee evening, freezing cold with a breeze from Lake Michigan that stopped you in your tracks. I recall wearing the warmest clothes that I packed for the trip, and the night air still cut through me as if I was naked.

The trip from Jordy's apartment to Butch's was a brief ten-minute ride, good thing as we were all excited to enjoy a legendary steak. The Butch's experience hit you the second you walked in the door. No one was there to greet you, and you were overcome by a full complement of bric-a-brac most likely to be seen at a local thrift shop.

We collectively made our own way through the museum-themed entrance until we were abruptly stopped by a woman with a heavy European accent and a noticeable limp. Her forty-plus years of smoking unfiltered Camels was prominent in her raspy voice and heavy breathing.

As she toiled to determine why we had entered her world on this evening, we were delivered to the dining room with the grace of a Walmart greeter, little passion accompanied by a wry smile.

The main room was filled with an abundance of charm and ambiance. Heavy curtains covered the windows, while the tables were adorned in red and white overlays. Each chair was different, and no two glasses matched. The room was filled with statues and eclectic paintings and sculptures. The only thing missing was Alfred Hitchcock.[9]

For a weekend night, the crowd was relatively sparse with only about half of the twenty or so tables occupied. We were offered a table in the middle of the room, but when we attempted to be seated, the table let forth an uncontrollable wobble, forcing us to select another location, this time closer to the back of the room.

Thank goodness!

As we settled into our new table for the evening, the joy and ease I felt being with Jordy and Jaclyn in the apartment had now drained from my being.

---

[9] Alfred Hitchcock (1899–1980), director, producer, and actor, known as the Master of Suspense (alfredhitchcock.com, life and legacy).

I had the sensation that every single person in the room was staring at me, wanting to know why the two beautiful young ladies sitting across from me were holding hands.

This was my first time in public with my daughter openly and cheerfully demonstrating her feelings for another woman. For what seemed like an eternity, we awaited our server and the chance to break the uncomfortable silence by ordering a much-needed round of cocktails.

To our chagrin, our waitress was the [10]Bella Lugosi–like matron that escorted us to our table. I recall thinking to myself this is the perfect prop in this horror-show evening.

Strangely and without conscious thought, the words from the Eagles' hit song "Hotel California" began playing in my head, *"You can check in any time you like but you can never leave."*

The menus were oversized dimensionally, and I sheepishly buried my entire body in the hope that everyone would return to their dinners and take their eyes off me and my wife, whom I discovered later felt very similar to me.

After studying the menu as if I was going to be tested, our waitress returned with the first of several challenging options for our dining experience.

In her brazen and unsympathetic tone, she announced that the bottle of wine that I had selected was not available and that she was going to bring us something better. The truth be told, the wine selection was broad, but the inventory was narrow. In essence, we were going to get what they had, not what we wanted.

Our drinks soon arrived, and we put our conversation on hold to make a toast.

The look in the eyes of my daughter told me that Jaclyn was different.

I believe they too had already realized this as well. To happiness! Cheers!

---

[10] Bella Lugosi (1882–1956), actor, famous for playing the role of Count Dracula, known as the King of Horror (belalugosi.com, legacy).

We had a lot to talk about since this was the first time that I had met Jaclyn. I could tell that she was different than the other young ladies that my daughter had dated in the recent past.

Jaclyn was older, mature, and very clear on her purpose and career path as a future collegiate head volleyball coach. She knew what she wanted and would pay whatever price necessary in order to live her dream.

Throughout the evening, the girls held hands albeit under the table. Above the surface they were consistently affectionate with each other, no different than any two heterosexual lovers in their twenties.

As the dinner progressed, I no longer saw two gay women. What had become apparent was that I was in the presence of two people in love, enjoying a wonderful evening filled with great food, drink, and companionship.

For me this transition from embarrassment to embracement was groundbreaking.

I am unsure at what point over the course of drinks, appetizers, dinner, and dessert that I abandoned whatever perceived opinion that the other patrons carried with them of the girls, my wife, and myself.

There are three things that last forever, faith, hope and love and the greatest of these is love.

(1 Corinthians 13:13, Holy Bible, NIV)

I had finally arrived at a place in my life where I was able to embrace love and nothing else mattered.

Dr. Wayne Dyer was famous for saying, *"When you change the way you look at things, the things you look at change."*

Fifty-plus years of judgment, bias, blame, discontent, and fear was wiped away in one magical evening. The only thing that remained were two beautiful souls that had found each other here on earth.

One Source

We are all spiritual beings having a human experience.

—Dr. Wayne Dyer
(paraphrasing Telihard de Chardin,
French Mystic 1881–1995)

Why in the world had I felt so confused, so conflicted, so unhappy with myself over learning the news of my daughter's sexual preference?

I was better than this, and I needed to continue to grow as a person. I needed to discover my real self, passion, and purpose.

It became evident that it was time for me to turn inward, to reevaluate my core beliefs, my feelings, and every aspect of my life that was made manifest by my thoughts.

The sages that walk among us that are consistently tethered to their universal source (God, Spirit, Way) would not have struggled to internalize the news of a daughter's same sex preference.

Those that have mastered their own souls would have warmly and energetically embraced the news, knowing that it was from source and it was the natural course of being for this individual.

No confusion, no conflict, no duality of thinking or being, just a knowing that we all emanate from One Source.

This source energy dwells in each of us, allows all of us access to one spirit, and manifests as light and love.

The universe has brought forth many teachers throughout the ages. However, what consistently emerged are 4 core beliefs to living a spiritual and joyous life.

Each sage, guru and master I encountered lived by a unique cultural and religious framework.

However, each of the masters returned to the same universal core beliefs necessary for us to understand one's road to self-discovery and spiritual enlightenment.

1. *Everything and everyone comes from One Source.*

   This Source has many names—*Spirit, God, Allah, Buddha, Yahweh, Krishna, Way, Intelligence,* and a litany of others based primarily on one's cultural or religious beliefs.

2. *In Source, we are One.*

   When we understand that we all emanate from One Source, we naturally come to the conclusion that we are all one in the same. We all share the exact same spiritual DNA.

3. *Source dwells within each one of us.*

   Through the daily practice of spiritual treatments, meditation, prayer, thought, silence, and many other techniques, we have the ability to draw from Source a heightened awareness of ourselves and the light and energy for living.

4. *Source is love.*

   When we arrive at the place that allows us to understand that everything in life emanates from love, we then have the opportunity to live as transparent, accepting, grateful, and mindful beings, capable of living in perfect peace.

Many of us will go through life never making the connection to the One Source, while others will only call upon source in times of sickness, poverty, or desperation.

The great teachers tell us that it is those individuals that understand the universal core beliefs, go within on a consistent basis, and remain connected throughout the day that have the best opportunity to harness wisdom and spiritual enlightenment on a consistent basis.

Everything and Everyone comes from One Source

The term universal intelligence was possibly first used by the Greek philosopher Anaxagoras 450BC. He introduced the idea of a Nous, the eternal mind, which transforms chaos into order and through it the material world comes into being. Anaxagoras (c. 500 BC- 428

BC), Pre- Socratic Greek Philosopher, (Stanford
Encyclopedia of Philosophy, published 8.22.2007
and revised in 10.1.2015)

*"In the beginning there was only intelligence or consciousness, creative
will, and universal energy. That was Source. Each human fragment-entity is a part of that Source. Whatever exists now, therefore, was created
by the will of that Source, using its intelligence, impressed upon the universal energy.*

*The intelligence of the Source is what we call the universal mind or
universal spirit. Mind is the evolving part of spirit. Each fragment-entity
is a part of that evolving universal mind and spirit.*

*The Source, or Creative Force, can only act out and exercise its
potential by thinking.*

*It uses its creative will to form thought images then impresses these
thought images upon the universal energy.*

*The thought images attract energy to them, and as the energy
vibrations slow down, the further away they travel from the originating
point, the thought images begin to solidify into matter, and the images
are transformed into physical forms. That is the way the physical-universe
system was created.*

*Nothing can manifest in this three-dimensional universe that did
not first exist in a mind, as a thought.*

*Nothing physical can materialize, exist, or evolve without conscious
thought by a spirit source. Nothing can happen by accident.*

*Our mind is the aspect of our spirit where all experiences that we
have had in all of time are recorded and maintained.*

*Mind is the attribute of spirit that stores information that stores
things that have existed in the past. It is the fragment-entity's connection
with the universal mind. This is how a person in regression, or other
altered states, can tune into past experiences.*

*We were fragmented to learn to use our mind to become cocreators
with the Source. The creations of every fragment-spirit must be able to
exist in balance and harmony with the creations of others. As a part of
this learning, we must also learn to dematerialize what we have materialized, also in balance and harmony with others.*

Unfortunately, or possibly fortunately, most entities in this time period cannot concentrate long enough on one thing, with enough intensity, to materialize their thought images. One day, however, all will have evolved to that point of creativity (the Nazarene way).

"Universal intelligence is in all matter and continually gives it all the properties and actions. So life becomes the union of intelligence and matter.

"Force unites intelligence and matter. Universal intelligence gives force to both inorganic and organic matter. That force which universal intelligence gives to organic matter as a higher order of its manifestations is called innate intelligence (organizing properties of living things)."

Hence through the power of this universal source (intelligence), the mind has the ability to manifest real world results by arranging random energy. Source gives us the ability to use our thoughts to produce tangible results.

It is acknowledged as fundamental universal intelligence, call it God if one must, *which is personified in man as innate intelligence; one of which is all intelligence, all powerful sufficient for the universe, the other of which is all powerful sufficient unto the unit, be that unit man or animal, insect or tree, etc., as exemplified in any, every and all living things.* (Volume 26, *Conflicts Clarify,* by B. J. Palmer, DC, PhC president, and the Palmer School of Chiropractic)

The more we are conscious of universal intelligence and connect ourselves to it, the more intelligence and wisdom we will have to work with. One might also describe Universal Intelligence as the mind of God or Spirit. (James Putnam, Universal Intelligence)

Takeaway: Through the divine power of One Great Source, we all originate from the exact same substance and energy.

At our birth, we all share the identical spiritual energy and intelligence. In the world, what ultimately separates us as we grow in body and mind is the religious and cultural beliefs that we are taught to be truths.

Our job is to return to source, to reconnect our mind, body, and spirit to our original way of being, our most natural state of existence, and to become who we are delivered here to be.

Tool: The next time you find yourself judging another person, become mindful and stop if you are capable. Ask yourself this question, since we are all from the same exact source, how can I be different from them?

The next time you experience great happiness or joy in your life, you are most certainly engaged in an activity, state of being or consciousness that you were brought here to manifest. If possible, ask yourself this question, do I feel connected to Source at this moment?

This experience is source flowing though you and out in the world and it is this One Source that is available for each of us to harness, to craft our best life each and every moment of every day.

On Children

Your children are not your children.
They are the sons and daughters
of Life's longing for itself.

They come through you but not from you,
And though they are with you yet
they belong not to you.

You may give them your love but not your thoughts,
For they have their own thoughts.

You may house their bodies but not their souls,
For their souls dwell in the house of tomorrow,
which you cannot visit, not even in your dreams.

You may strive to be like them,
But seek not to make them like you.
For life goes not backward nor tarries yesterday.

You are the bows from which your children
As living arrows are sent forth.

The archer seeks the mark upon the path of the
infinite, and He bends you with his might
That His arrows may go swift and far.
Let your bending in the archer's
hand be for the gladness;
For even as He loves the arrow that flies,
so He loves also the bow that is stable.

Kahlil Gibran, 1883–1931, Lebanese
Philosopher and writer

In Source, We Are All One

Ramana Maharshi (1879–1950), an Indian sage who his devotees
credit with being the father of self-enquiry, which is the continual
attention to one's inner awareness the real self or "I," said it best when
he shared his unprecedented depth of enlightenment by stating,

"There are no others."

> *He maintained that the real "self" is always pres-
> ent and always experienced but he emphasized that
> one is only consciously aware of it as it really is when
> the self-limiting tendencies of the mind have ceased.
> Permanent and continuous Self-Awareness is known as
> self- realization.* (sriramanamaharshi.org)

> *Ramana's primary methodology for teaching his devo-
> tees the art of self- awareness was to realize the self or
> "I" through the practice of silence. He who lives only for
> himself, creating a web of desires, becomes entangled in
> those webs. But he that acts and works for God (source) is
> free. You do not know why you are on earth, or why you
> are a man or a woman, or why you are the way you are.*
> *You are here to do God's (source) will.*
> *To work for you is to be bound by life.*
> *To work for God (source) is to be free.*
> (Paramahansa Yogananda, Journey to Self-Realization)

75

Takeaway: Silence is golden.

By turning inward and becoming quiet, you have the ability to become one with your own true thoughts. It is here that you can consciously determine the thoughts that are negative and self-defeating and hence banish. At the same time, you can embrace the thoughts that have the ability to assist you in the creation of a positive and successful mind-set.

It is here in a silent, quiet, meditative state that one has the ability to consciously connect with source, and it is here that you gain an understanding of what is necessary to be yourself and to live the life you were intended to live.

Tool: Discover your place of peace.

Schedule yourself a minimum of fifteen minutes each day. I carve out one hour in the morning before I start my workday. Find a place to be alone. Mine is a parking spot on a tree-lined road about five minutes from my workplace. It is here that I read inspiring literature or the Bible, write in my journal, or just close my eyes and turn inward.

Do whatever inspires you and fosters your ability to think and luxuriate in your own dreams, goals, and desires of your heart.

Practice this daily and watch how you joyfully become a person who can consciously stay connected to source throughout the day.

As crazy as it sounds, over time you will understand what Ramana meant by "There are no others." As we become a person soulfully connected to everything and everyone, you will begin to practice being grateful, forgiving, humble, and filled with love and humility.

The world you have the opportunity to experience will not exist in duality—white or black, rich or poor, straight or gay. You are free to discover and enjoy everything and everyone in the same light.

Oneness is the perfect expansion of our inner reality.
Let our heart's oneness only increase
To make us feel

That we belong to a universal world, family,
And this world family
Is a fulfilled Dream of God.

(Sri Chinmoy)[11]

Source Dwells within Each One of Us

Source is not something that you can access externally. Source exists inside each of us and only by turning inward can we discover and use this powerful energy for our well-being and self-discovery.

Paramanhansa Yoganada, the great Indian yogi, *"defined self-realization as 'the knowing in body, mind and soul that we are one with the omnipresence of God (Source, Universal Source, Spirit); that all we have to do is improve our knowing."*

So the magical question is, "How do we improve our knowing?"

Realizing we are all from the same source, understanding that this source exists inside each of us, it is our lifetime journey to become conscious of the all-powerful and all-present source. Our passionate pursuit leads us to truly know that we have arrived at our original place of being in this world.

It is by being at this place on a consistent basis that we will understand who we are and what it is we are intended to do with our life.

In reality, I had a lot of work to do on me.

As the great Dr. Dyer is fond of saying, *"The door to enlightenment opens inward."*

St. Augustine writes, *"But you were more* inward *than my own inwardness"* (Confessions 3.6.11).

*"God (source) is not to be sought outside the self, for God (source) is already there **within**, eternally more intimate to me that I am to myself"* (St Augustine and Self Discovery, "The darkness of God: Negativity in Christian Mysticism, p.59).

---

[11]   Sri Chinmoy (1931–2007) Indian writer and guru; A spiritual teacher who dedicated his life in service to aspiring humanity. (www.srichinmoy.com)

The Johnny Lee hit "Looking for Love" best describes the sadness of a person that chooses to search for love externally instead of, turning inward and listening to the voice of the heart (soul, source).

Hopin' to find a friend and a lover, I'll bless the day I discover, Another heart lookin' for love.

Takeaway: We go through life focused on the things in the external world. We pursue the pleasures of the flesh, existing to please others, seeking approval, accolades, and wealth, all the while protecting a man-made reputation.

Why?

To measure up to some preexisting threshold of success, allowing the EGO (edging God out) to dictate our words and actions, all the while ignoring source and our natural state of being.

Take the time each day to turn inward and connect with your true self and live the life you were created to live.

Tool: The next time you feel yourself having a desire for something of this world, a new suit, a car, or perhaps a bigger house, close your eyes and feel the way you would if you had that thing you wanted. Can you feel a true joy and experience pleasure just by the feeling of the wish fulfilled? If you cannot, then this is an external desire. If you can, this is something of the heart. Embrace the feeling. Now let it go.

Source Is Love

Source is energy. Love is energy. Source is love.

Love exists as the highest form of energy. Physics tells us that energy vibrates at variable frequencies. Love is said to vibrate at the highest frequency.

Those who live in love vibrate at a much-higher frequency than those that do not. A lack of love allows for the worldly energy of a lower vibratory nature to penetrate a person. When this occurs, positivity turns to negativity, faith to fear, happiness to sadness, and worst of all, love to hate.

The key is to stay in conscious contact with source energy. The longer we can remain connected, the stronger our love will be. Our society is made up of individuals that are on all levels of source frequencies.

Success, prosperity, abundance, favor, and good health all flow from the attachment to source energy and the detachment to worldly desires and materialistic conditional thinking.

> *When the power of LOVE*
> *Replaces the love of power*
> *Man will have a new name: God.* (Sri Chinmoy)

Takeaway:

> *Love is patient, love is kind. It does not envy, it does not boast, it is not proud.*
>
> *It does not dishonor others, it is not self-seeking, it is not easily angered, and it keeps no record of wrongs.*
>
> *Love does not delight in evil but rejoices with the truth.*
>
> *It always protects, always trusts, always hopes, and always perseveres.*
>
> *Love never fails.*
>
> *"But where there are prophecies, they will cease; where there are tongues, they will be stilled; where there is knowledge, it will pass away."* (Corinthians 13:4–8, Holy Bible, New International Version [NIV])

Tool: When an issue arises, get still and meditate (think) on source (God, love), remain in a state of highly conscience thought of source (God, love), and in a very short period of time, the issue at hand will dissolve.

Let Go and Let God.

THE 80'S

Life is one grand sweet song, so start the music.

—Ronald Reagan
(40th President of the United States, 1911–2004)

In hindsight, the eighties were a pivotal decade of growth for the gay and lesbian community both here in the United States and across the globe.

The eighties were marked by great adversity, and none greater than the HIV/AIDS emergence and epidemic. It was also a time that bore witness to the US Supreme Court's ruling that there was no fundamental right to be gay.

Across the pond, Margret Thatcher's government drafted clause 28, making it illegal for the local authorities to provide or garner any type of support that might promote homosexual relationships as a viable alternative to the heterosexual family life.

The small fan at the base of my feet was rotating left to right while humming relentlessly. I was sprawled out on a lumpy mattress, no box spring or frame, and wondered what the day ahead would bring. I had just arrived in Ocean City, Maryland, for the summer fresh off my plebe year at West Point.

It was June 1980, and my life as a nonmilitary adult was about to begin. I was invited to live with my childhood best friend and his buddies from high school on 128th Street on the ocean side adjacent to Coastal Highway. There were six of us in a three-bedroom condo, and the room that I was assigned did not have windows, basically a walk-in closet with two single beds on the floor and an area to store some clothing.

As you can imagine, we did not have enough money to turn on the air-conditioning, so the little electric portable fan was my only vehicle for moving the stale, beer-infused air from one side of the room to the other.

Ocean City, is a small resort town that is bordered between the Atlantic Ocean and Assawoman Bay. As a child, my family would spend one week per year here on vacation. Complete with my mother, father, sister, and sometimes grandmother (Dad's father passed away when I was five), we would make the annual pilgrimage in an attempt to cram an entire summer of fun into seven days.

I was twenty years old, working as a stock boy at a Drug Fair, making less than one hundred dollars per week. Believe it or not, I still managed to save twenty bucks a week, which was promptly delivered every Friday to the Home Bank Savings and Loan.

Thirty-eight years ago, Drug Fair was one of the largest regional retail chains of drugstores in the country.

So how did I manage to live on eighty dollars per week? Keep in mind the rent was paid for the summer, and I was not married nor did I have any children. Normally I ate one and a half meals a day, which combined totaled no more than five dollars (seven times five is thirty-five dollars), and electric bill was ten dollars per month, which left me thirty-five dollars a week for beer.

As working stiffs, we normally only went out three nights a week, Wednesday to the family fish house for ladies' night and Friday and Saturday to enjoy the weekend when our family or friends from the old neighborhood came to visit. We knew where to go to drink all night for eight to ten dollars. Oh, the good old days.

Having spent the last two summers shooting an M16 rifle, firing an M60 machine gun, becoming efficient on the hand grenade range, and learning how to properly don a chemical suit to ward off the hazards of a gas attack, I had no issues with the day-to-day mundane tasks that awaited me as a stock boy.

Since I left for the Army in June 1978, I wore a uniform every day except when I was on vacation and away from school. When I arrived at the beach, I had a few pairs of army-issue khaki pants, some basic short-sleeve shirts, a few pairs of shorts, and one bathing suit. To say the least not exactly a wardrobe designed for a full summer at the beach.

I arrived on Sunday, June 1, and immediately joined the boys in an evening of ballyhoo and tomfoolery. Hence, reporting for work at 9:00 a.m. on Monday was no picnic. I dressed in, of course, khaki pants, a blue short-sleeve button-down shirt, and brown loafers, resembling a prep schooler heading off for the first day of school.

Still sporting a military haircut, I in no way looked like any of my friends, who were seasoned beach bums. The store manager, and my boss, was a grizzled, chain-smoking Vietnam veteran with a solid case of Post-traumatic-stress-disorder. I could tell we would get along just fine when he learned of my military background and my prowess for mopping floors and using the industrial buffer to make the store's aisles shine like they never had in the past.

There was something about this place that I really liked—the slow pace, the mindless tasks, and the sense of accomplishment in stocking a shelf or cleaning the restrooms. No one was yelling at me, and no one expected me to be in formation at 0500 for physical training. I was a young again. I was me.

Several weeks into my stint at Drug Fair, a group of very attractive young ladies, all recent high school graduates, joined our team for the summer. This group of girls was unlike any other I had ever had the opportunity to know in high school, prep school, or at West Point.

Having lived a relatively shallow and sheltered existence to this point in my life, I had really never met or had the privilege to get to know girls that were from upper-socioeconomic families and of the Jewish faith. This bunch was different and one of these girls would change the course of my life forever.

As with many things in life, time quickly revealed to me why I was destined to leave the academy. It was to meet my soul mate, Lori Weinberger.

Lori was and remains to this day a physically attractive lady. At the ripe old age of eighteen, Lori was easy on the eyes, and I became attracted to her almost immediately. Reporting for work one day, I first noticed her perched up in the manager overwatch at the front of the store. It seems that Lori's father's best friend knew some folks at the home office of Drug Fair and secured for Lori a bookkeeper-like position.

Unlike the rest of us that stocked shelves, ran a cash register, or cleaned the store, this position of privilege allowed her not to have to engage in the menial tasks like the rest of us while being paid about twice as much.

As it turns out, Lori also made notice of the khaki-wearing, military-clad preppy who was working at Drug Fair, and it appears the attraction was mutual. As we liked to say in the Army, it was a target-rich environment, and the summer had just begun.

Our first date occurred just days after we discovered each other at Drug Fair. We decided that we would go for a drink one late afternoon to Fagers Island.

A local landmark, Fagers Island is a bayside bar and restaurant on Sixtieth Street serving up great food, cocktails and sunsets from anywhere on their multiple-tiered decks. As detailed earlier, my financial situation was a bit strained at the time, so this date was planned very carefully by me.

It was a beautiful early evening around 4:00 p.m., so happy hour had just begun. We were seated immediately at a wonderful table with a great view of the bay and the bridge that carried beach enthusiast to and from the barrier island.

Our waitress was attentive, and I quickly ordered two house drafts for us both at, happy hour prices. I made every attempt to nurse my beer, but one can only take so long to drink a twelve-ounce draft.

To Lori and the waitress's surprise, I requested the check after we both had enjoyed our beverage. Each beer was priced at two dollars, hence leaving me one dollar for a tip. Yes, folks, that's right, how to successfully go on a date for five dollars (circa 1980).

I got the sense that Lori expected our visit to Fagers Island to last a little longer than it actually did. However, the night was just beginning. We headed back in Lori's sports car to my humble abode and made a beeline down to the beach for an evening stroll and that fate-filled first kiss. Little did we know that our kiss on that evening would last thirty-eight-plus years and bless us with two wonderful children.

U of MD , College Park

When summer ended, we both headed off to the University of Maryland at College Park. Once again as fate would have it, we were both assigned to the same coed dormitory and separated by just two floors. Clearly this was a sign that we were meant to be together, as the odds of that occurring were extremely slim.

Our time passed rapidly at UMD from fall 1980 to summer 1981, and the next thing you know we were back at the beach for another summer of sun and fun!

This time a little older and a bit wiser but not any better off financially, at least for me. We resumed our old jobs at Drug Fair and settled in for another summer of parties, listening to local bands, lounging on the beach, and just enjoying time away from the books.

Summers turned to fall, falls to winters, and winters to springs, and all too soon our journey at the University of Maryland, College Park, would come to a glorious crescendo on May 23, 1983. Graduation day was wonderful, thousands of black-robed-and-capped eager, young, intelligent, and excited young men and women ready to go forth and make their mark on the world, and I was one of them.

This was an especially special day in the Kirr family as I was the first Kirr to graduate from a four-year college. This degree bequeathed me this day, a bachelor of science, BS mathematical, physical science, and engineering, was mine to use as I set forth into the world, with all rights and privileges bestowed.

I recall the day like it was yesterday, surrounded by my mother, Helen; father, William; and sister, Renee. We were joined as well by my newly minted fiancée, Lori, and of course her mother, Dolores, and father, Hal.

The day was perfect. Blue skies and bright sunshine presented the perfect backdrop for our unfortunately indoor commencement ceremony, held at the Cole Field House.

Dr. John B. Slaughter, chancellor, College Park campus, delivered the speech that released us out into the working world. Honestly, I do not recall one word of the speech, only that it seemed to last a lifetime. It was hot, and I was hungry and, to be brutally honest, a bit hungover as we enjoyed the final night at the Delta Tau Delta fraternity house in style.

Directly following the graduation ceremony, Hal and Dolores were kind enough to treat myself and my family for a lunch celebration at the Rusty Scupper, a waterfront restaurant perfectly situated across the way from Harborplace, Baltimore, Maryland complete with a breathtaking view.

I still recall how proud my parents were that day and how good I felt about my personal accomplishment, goal set, a long journey traveled, and the finish line was bittersweet. The college days were now officially in the rearview mirror. It was time to take the next steps in this thing called life.

I recall not even letting the ink on my diploma dry before I was working full-time for my father-in-law's manufacturer's representative firm. Our company represented multiple lines of office furniture in the mid-Atlantic region. Our role was to market and sell each company's products to office furniture retailers, office supply stores, designers, and architectural firms that specified furniture for their clients.

Our furniture companies made wood desks, wood chairs, steel desks and metal seating, ergonomic seating, metal filing cabinets, storage cabinets, and even furniture designed exclusively for this new thing that began to pop up on every single office desk in the country, a personal computer, or PC.

Little did I know that I was about to experience the explosion of technology that would change the world forever. I was twenty-three years old and at the origin of the personal computer revolution.

In 1976, Steve Jobs and Steve Wozniak started Apple computer in the garage of Job's family and on April Fool's Day, they rolled out Apple I, with a single circuit board.

In 1977, Jobs and Wozniak incorporated Apple and showed the Apple II at the first West Coast computer fair.

In 1981, IBM introduced its first personal computer, the Acorn. The product was sold exclusively through Sears and ComputerLand and popularized the term PC.

By the time I graduated from the University of Maryland in 1983, Apple introduced the Lisa, which was the first personal computer with [12]graphical user interface.

It eventually evolved into the Macintosh.

Wedding Bells

On January 28, 1984, Lori and I were married. Yes, just eight months after graduation and at the ripe old ages of twenty and twenty-three, we embarked on our journey together, now as husband and wife. As crazy as this sounds today, it was not uncommon for young men and women in their early twenties to tie the knot.

Our wedding was anything but conventional, Lori being from the Jewish faith and I, Catholic. Our ceremony was officiated by a rabbi and a priest. Our two families could not have been more different, Lori's parents and family were from New York, primarily Brooklyn and Queens, and my family from Dundalk, Maryland. The Weinbergers were wealthy, and the Kirrs from the lower-socioeconomic rung of society.

On the surface, this had the makings for a potentially awkward and uncomfortable affair. I can honestly say that it was neither. Our host for the evening was none other than Martin Resnick, the owner of Martin's catering and banquet facilities and personal friend to Hal and Dolores.

One of the fortunate by-products of an interfaith marriage is that you can perform the ceremony in the same building as the reception, so once we exchanged vows, the doors opened, and our guests were able to spill out into the room where the cocktail hour would take place. The party was epic.

Hal and Dolores spared no expense. The cocktail hour alone was incredible. As a matter of fact, several of my relatives thought that this was the primary function and ate and drank so much that

---

[12] *"Graphical user interface allows users to interact with electronic devices through graphical icons and visual indicators such as secondary notation, as opposed to text-based interfaces, typed command labels or text navigation"* (Wikipedia).

when the doors opened up to the next room where the principal part of the reception was to take place, they already had their fill. However, I have a funny feeling they found room for the surf and turf that was soon to be served and the mountain of desserts that capped off the evening.

The entertainment for the evening was a twenty-piece orchestra from New York, as Dolores wanted to make sure they could play "New York, New York," a Sinatra hit and her favorite. They were phenomenal, as their music energized both cultures with Jewish and Italian favorites.

Dolores had specifically told Marty Resnick and the Martin's staff to please attempt to accommodate all the guests' wishes. Well, there's always one willing to test the waters. Upon learning of this decree, Ron Ercolano, who was a guest but also worked for Martin's as a maître d', requested a dozen steamed crabs. In short order, the crabs arrived in all their glory, and our guests, clad in formal wear, ate steamed crabs at our wedding reception.

The wedding was perfect, complete with my beautiful bride and her lovely bridesmaids adorned with bouquets of long-stemmed roses with baby breath. Everyone got along, everyone mixed and mingled, and for one magical night, everyone put aside their differences and came together to celebrate the love that two people had confessed to each other on that evening. Given the opportunity love has the power to unite.

Hal and Dolores poured out their heart and demonstrated their love for us by creating an affair that I can honestly say is the very best wedding I have ever attended, and many others to this day share my sentiments. What occurred that night cannot be overlooked. The miracle of love was present, and Jew and Gentile alike basked in its warmth.

Upon our return from our honeymoon in Acapulco, Mexico, Lori and I settled in to our life as Mr. and Mrs. Stephen Kirr. We had it all. Lori had a terrific position with the investment banking company T. Rowe Price, working in the institutional bond department for some of the brightest minds in the financial world. Hal had brought me on as a young salesman in the furniture representative business. Life was good.

> *There is an Indian proverb or axiom that says everyone is a house with 4 rooms, a physical, a mental, an emotional and a spiritual. Most of us tend to live in one room most of the time but unless we go into every room every day, even if only to keep it aired, we are not a complete person.* (Rumer Godden, *A House with Four Rooms*)

My wife gave birth to our son, Adam, on July 13, 1986, and after our daughter, Jordyn (Jordy), followed on March 4, 1989. However, only by the grace of God did my life not abruptly end on the evening of November 30, 1988.

I remember the day as if it were yesterday. I had a sales manager in town from an office furniture company that I represented in the area. We began our day at the crack of dawn with client breakfast, lunch, and dinner appointments beginning in Maryland and culminating in downtown Washington, DC, at the Prime Rib restaurant.

As was customary back in the day, and perhaps even still today, the steaks came accompanied by a few bottles of wine. Realizing I had to drive back to Baltimore that evening, I was very responsible with my consumption.

Once the dinner was complete, it was after 10:00 p.m., with a one-hour drive still to be executed and then another thirty minutes from the downtown Baltimore hotel of my guest to my home in the country.

I recall being okay when I dropped off my guest just after 11:00 p.m. at the Marriott hotel across the street from Camden Yards, but as I made the drive back to my home, fatigue hit me hard. In an attempt to stay awake, I opened my driver's side window to allow as much November night air to battle the long day of driving, meeting, entertaining, and overeating.

I did well. Everything seemed to be working fine as I entered the home stretch of my trip, but as I made the left hand turn on to my street, I must have let my body relax, my eyes closed for what seemed like a split second, and the next thing I know, I was heading directly into the path of a telephone poll, luckily now only going about twenty miles an hour.

The impact of my Audi detonated the airbag and ultimately saved my life. When I came to, the front of the car was completely collapsed right up to the front window, and I was amazed to find that I did not have one noticeable scratch on my body.

Unable to open any of the doors, I crawled out of the front passenger-side window and walked the less than one mile to my home. Clearly dazed and confused, I entered the house and woke my wife from her slumber. You can only imagine her reaction to seeing me stand there with my disheveled clothes, blood now running down my forehead from a slight cut and realizing that I should have just died in a single-person car crash.

My wife, realizing that I had left the scene of an accident, immediately called our next-door neighbor who was an attorney and asked for his advice. He advised us to return to the scene as soon as possible and call the police.

By the time we arrived back at the scene, the police were already there. They asked if I was okay, to which I said I was, and they wanted to know if I needed medical attention, which I did not. The car was removed, and my wife and I returned home.

I should have known right then and there that God had a much-larger purpose for my life; it was now up to me to discover exactly what that purpose would be.

I had it all—a beautiful family, a good career, health, family, and friends. From the outside, all appeared perfect, but like a duck, above the surface of the water, I was cool, calm, and collected, but underneath the waterline I was paddling like hell!

At the ripe old age of twenty-nine, I had a wife, two children, a business, a mortgage, credit card debt, car payments, insurance, college-saving responsibility, a wedding (in twenty-six years) to fund, as well anything and everything else that goes with being fully immersed in the material world.

Reflecting back on this time in my life, I can honestly say I purely existed. I clearly had become devoid of any real mental, emotional, or spiritual growth or enlightenment. I knew that there was more to life than the physical world that I had become enslaved; I needed to explore and expand my mental, emotional, and spiritual IQ.

I began to study the masters and search for the true meaning of my existence. One of my favorites was Tony Robbins, a young, gregarious, GQ-looking new-age Zen master from San Diego. I became so engrossed in his works that I actually flew out to California one weekend to meet with him along with a group of about eighteen others. Over the course of the weekend, we were introduced to Tony's new business model, a franchise that allowed Anthony Robbins trained personnel to conduct field training utilizing his personal mastery system.

One of the mantras from Tony's teachings was, *"If your life is worth living, it is worth recording"*

I began to journal and to pour out my most intimate feelings on to the paper. Some of my journaling is mundane and not of interest, but other recordings are extremely insightful and display my depth and range of emotions at each step of my life.

Allow me to share some milestone comments, each one my own and each one will allow you to get a glimpse into my heart and soul as I grew from a young man to a father of two brides.

Journal Dedication

This record is dedicated to my wife, Lori, and my children, Adam and Jordyn. May these thoughts whenever read provide for them a better understanding of why and how I lived my life.

My first Entry

Q. Who am I?
"When the student is ready, the teacher appears."
I am a human being who from this day forward is committed to making my life an example and not a warning. I am committed to a passion inside of me to help those who cannot help themselves.

Note: Man's behavior is congruent with his or her identity. Therefore, one will act in accordance with how one feels about him or herself.

"I feel that I AM a spiritual being having a human experience" (Dr. Wayne Dyer).

Note: I believe that one must live to grow and give. We as humans begin to die as soon as we are born. Our life can be expressed as a parenthesis in eternity.

Eternity------(our life opens----we live----we die)-----eternity

We can never own anybody or anything (a touch of foreshadowing as I will profess this the night Jordy comes out some twenty-one years later).

It is our purpose to give every human being we encounter more value in his or her life. We must process life with an attitude of abundance not scarcity.

I am excited about today's events. I had an opportunity to attend a birthday party with my children and then later that evening being able to spend time with good friends at an art auction. Life is what you make it. I am making my life a wonderful experience.

Note to family: Children, set your goals, then devise your plan of action to achieve your goals. But most importantly, act out your plan with vigor and passion. For without action, nothing can be won or lost. Always look inside yourself for new and unique ways to grow and to add value to the lives of others.

The world was changing, barriers were coming down, and people all around the world were taking the actions necessary that would lead to gays and lesbians ultimately having the opportunity to openly express their love for one another.

Love thy neighbor, and treat each other as you would wish to be treated.

The 80's

LGBTQ Milestones

➢ On July 8, 1980, the democratic rules committee states that it will not discriminate against homosexuals. At their national convention on August 11-14, the Democrats become the first political party to endorse a homosexual rights platform. (Timeline: Milestones in the American Gay Rights Movement, PBS.org)

➢ On July 3, 1981, the New York Times prints the first story of a rare pneumonia and skin cancer found in 41 gay men in New York and California. The CDC initially refers to the disease as GRID, Gay Related Immune Deficiency Disorder. When the symptoms are found outside of the gay community, Bruce Voeller, biologist and founder of the National Gay Task Force, success-fully lobbies to change the name of the disease to AIDS. (Timeline: Milestones in the American Gay Rights Movement, PBS.org)

➢ March 2, 1982, Wisconsin becomes the first state to outlaw discrimination on the basis of sexual orienta-tion. (Timeline: Milestones in the American Gay Rights Movement, PBS.org)

➢ In 1983 researchers discover the virus (Human Immunodeficiency Virus or HIV) that causes AIDS. (USC.edu)

➢ In 1984 Boston Mayor Raymond Flynn signs an execu-tive order protecting gays in city employment.

➢ 1984, The city of Berkley, California City Council passes a domestic partnership bill granting equal benefits to long term gay and unmarried heterosexual couples. (USC.edu)

➢ 1984, West Hollywood, California incorporates and a majority of openly gay City Council members are elected, making it the first gay- run city. (USC.edu)

➢ Ireland, Brazil, and France made history by legally granting rights to all those in the LGBT community. All in all around the globe there were over 125 separate laws changed in favor of the gay and lesbian community in the 1980s.

IOWA V. MARYLAND

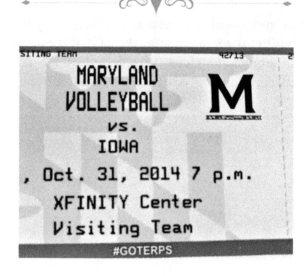

SITING TEAM   42713   2

**MARYLAND
VOLLEYBALL**
M
vs.
IOWA
, Oct. 31, 2014 7 p.m.
XFINITY Center
Visiting Team

#GOTERPS

As an assistant coach for the Iowa Hawkeyes, Jaclyn was in town.

Several weeks before, Jaclyn had probed Lori and I as to determine our ability to attend this game against our alma mater.

As a graduate of the University of Maryland and a varsity lacrosse player, I was no stranger to the athletic facilities that graced the friendly confines of College Park. However, since graduation in May 1983, I had returned sparingly but always supportive of my terrapins.

As Lori and I arrived on campus that brisk October evening, we were amazed at all the wonderful changes that had taken place over the many years. The front entrance was reconfigured, the main road lined with fresh new architecture, while high-tech labs and research facilities adorned the chemistry, biology, and physics buildings.

I felt such a sense of pride as I parked the car behind the magnificent Xfinity Center, but tonight was unique. I would be rooting against my beloved red and white. Tonight my allegiance belonged to Jaclyn and her black-and-gold Iowa Hawkeyes.

This was first volleyball match that Lori and I had ever attended in our lives. We did not know what to expect nor did we realize that we would be watching the first of many more matches in our lives.

As we entered into the arena, you could feel the energy and the buzz that comes only from a live sporting event. We made our way to the will call ticket area to pick up our free passes and were kindly redirected over to the Iowa booth. Oops, forgot where are allegiance was for the evening.

Just as we picked up our tickets and were heading toward the volleyball arena entrance, I spotted Jaclyn coming down the hallway. As usual, she looked beautiful, radiating that wholesome Midwestern glow and smiling like a Cheshire cat.

It was about thirty minutes before the match would begin, and we took time to visit with Jaclyn, keeping the pregame banter light and closing with the promise to spend some time visiting after the match ended.

Clearly Jaclyn had something to tell my wife and I as her tonality and body language suggested much more than a simple postmatch wrap-up chat.

Since it was a Friday evening, and Halloween to add, the gym was charged with terrapin pride and electricity and very well attended.

When the first set began, I immediately could tell that I would embrace the sport. The women athletes were imposing with the front line players averaging over six feet coupled with a jumping ability like I had never witnessed.

As the below edited press release reveals, the Terps were no match for the well-coached and extremely athletic Hawkeyes.

HAWKEYES TAKE THREE SETS
OVER TERRAPINS

COLLEGE PARK, Md.–The Maryland volleyball team fell in straight sets (21–25, 17–25, 20–25) to Iowa Friday evening in the XFINITY Center Pavilion.

"I thought Iowa competed really hard tonight," said head coach Steve Aird. I thought they were well prepared and their coaching staff did a great job of getting them ready to play. . . . I think our team is learning what it takes to win in this conference."

"I think we did some nice things at times, just not consistent enough to give us a shot to win the match."

The teams played a close first set to start the match. Maryland recorded 4.5 total blocks in the first set as the game was tied 10 times and the lead changed five times.

The Hawkeyes would go on to take the first set, 25–21.

In the second set, both teams had nine kills in the game, the set once again featured 10 ties, with the final tie coming at 15. Iowa was able to take advantage of Maryland attack errors, and a service ace gave the Hawkeyes the set win and a 2–0 match lead going into intermission.

In another close set, Maryland was able to take an early lead from the Hawkeyes.

Iowa took the lead back off attack errors allowing the Hawkeyes to increase the lead to 25–20 and take the match in three sets." (www.umterps.com/ Maryland Athletics/Volleyball)

I can honestly attest that I had very mixed emotions about the Hawkeyes win over my beloved Terrapins. This feeling lasted only a brief moment as I embraced the fact that my daughter's girlfriend was the coach of the winning team.

After the match ended, the court was almost immediately and completely engulfed by players, parents, fans, media, and Maryland students coming to the aid of their friends on the team providing empathy and support to their hometown ladies.

Once the Iowa players had shaken the hands of the opposing Terrapins, and the coaches had offered the media their take on the match, we were able to finally meet with Jaclyn and her head coach, Bond Shamansky.

Both Bond and Jaclyn were beaming from ear to ear as their Hawkeyes had just dismantled a Big Ten opponent 3–0 to win the match. Bond is a very fit and stylish person, and very confident in his coaching abilities. He was gracious in his postgame chitchat but was abruptly taken away by yet another media person looking for additional perspective from the winning head coach.

Jaclyn walked us away from the midcourt commotion and away from almost everyone else in the arena. After a little bit more small talk, Jaclyn got to the words that she was waiting to deliver all evening.

"I would like to ask Jordy to marry me." The words were said in a fashion of requesting permission and with a warm and gentle sweetness.

We were thrilled. In no time flat, our feelings for Jaclyn had escalated to great heights. We knew that Jordy's journey for lifelong companionship had culminated when she met and embraced Jaclyn Simpson.

Jordy and Jaclyn were and are soul mates!

The Iowa women's volleyball team flies on a private chartered plane. That's right, this fact alone demonstrates just how big women's volleyball is in the Midwest. We visited for a few more minutes, but the Hawkeyes were eager to get out of College Park, get those wheels up, and get back to Iowa City as quickly as they possibly could.

Our goodbye embraces were extra special, as this was no longer someone that Jordy dated, as time would tell she was to be our daughter-in-law in relatively short order.

Jaclyn was exhausted and elated a winner on and off the court; the future was certainly beginning to round into shape.

As Lori and I exited the Xfinity Center, the cool late October air bit through our outer wear. We held each other's hand feeling the heaviness of the long workweek come to a crashing crescendo now coupled with the reality that we would be responsible for a wedding sometime within the next year or so.

These were the best of times; these were the worst of times. Truth be told that we never really saved specifically for Jordy's wedding. We have provided both of our children with everything they ever wanted and more, private high schools and college education, with no student loans to pay back upon graduation, cars, vacations, and plenty of spending money.

Now don't get me wrong, we have saved for our own retirement, endowed an emergency fund, and always had plenty of available dollars to pay the bills and enjoy our lives without much of a struggle. We were blessed, or so we thought.

October 31, 2014, and we were officially in wedding mode. For those of you that have married off either a son or daughter, you know exactly what I mean. Every conversation from now until they turn off the lights at the reception will eventually lead to some aspect of the planning process.

For the next twenty months of our lives, we would talk about nothing else but venues, flowers, bands, table composition, food, drink, friends, relatives, weather, dresses, tuxedos, favors, bachelorette parties, and of course, the budget.

I had a budget in mind, my daughter had a budget in mind, and my wife had a budget in mind, and what are the odds that any of them matched. Not only did they not match, they were not even in the same ballpark. Clearly I was mistaken to think that one could have a lovely wedding for the same price you could buy a new home for in 1980.

A friend of mine likes to compare a wedding reception to a day in which you go out and purchase your favorite automobile, drive it, take some photos, and enjoy it immeasurably for six hours and then send it over a cliff, with nothing to show for it but a few photos and some memories.

The good news was that we had a year-and-half-plus to put away the money that would be necessary to make our daughter's wedding one that both bride and mother would agree was simply magical.

As fathers can attest, it is very difficult to say no to your little girl. My situation was even more unique. I was the Father 4 the Bridez.

Jaclyn was raised by her mother, Cheryl, and her grandmother Betty. Knowing this fact, I willingly wanted to be received as that loving, caring, and supportive male in her life.

My entire being was to simply love her as much as I love my own children, and that is certainly how I feel this very day.

THE 90'S

Every man dies, not every man lives.

—William Wallace, The Movie *Braveheart*, 1995

By the time I was thirty, I was a mess, and no one knew it but me. Sure, on the outside, everything looked great. I had a loving wife, two healthy children, (ages four and one), a beautiful house in the country, my own manufacturer's representative firm, both sets of parents, a loving sister, and plenty of friends to socialize with on the weekends.

At the ripe old age of thirty, I was squarely ensconced on the hamster's wheel. At a time when most young men and women were either just really starting their professional careers, still dating, or just getting married, my wife and I had been married for six years, had two babies, a mortgage, a business, and all the self-induced stress you can imagine.

It was here in the early 1990s that I earnestly began to search my heart and soul in an effort to determine what I really wanted to do with this one life that was bestowed upon me by our creator and one source.

June 30, 1990, my dearest wife, Lori, threw me a thirtieth surprise birthday party at BOP (Brick Oven Pizza) located in downtown Baltimore in the Fells Point neighborhood. The party was a blast complete with beer, pizza, family, and friends.

Once again, I had everything but my soul.

I must admit, I think that Charles Dickens said it best back in 1859 when in his work *A Tale of Two Cities* he so famously pens the following:

> *It was the best of times, it was the worst of times, it was the age of wisdom, it was the age of foolishness, it was the epoch of belief, it was the epoch of incredulity, it was the season of light, it was a season of darkness, it was*

the spring of hope, it was the winter of despair, we had everything before us, we had nothing before us, we were all going direct to heaven, we were all going direct the other way. (Quotations page.com/Charles Dickens, A Tale of Two Cities, 1859)

In 1990, at a time when Nelson Mandela got released from prison in South Africa and became the leader of the ANC, East and West Germany were reunited, and we bore witness the collapse of the Soviet Union (thepeoplehistory.com).

In 1991, the red ribbon is adopted as the symbol of awareness and compassion for those living with HIV/AIDS.

The dichotomy of success and failure during this decade is simply astonishing; personally Lori and I were having a great time raising the children. However, in 1991, the US economy slowed, and we entered into a time of economic downturn.

"This global recession came swiftly after the Black Monday of October 1987, resulting from a stock collapse of the Dow Jones Industrial Average of 22.6%" (thebubblebubble.com, Black Monday- the Stock Market Crash of 1987, by Jesse Colombo 8.3.2012).

These turn of events were the catalyst that precipitated us making the decision to sell our home in the country and move in with my in-laws for six months while we built a new home.

Our new home was located at the end of a quiet cul-de-sac in a brand-new development that came complete with a community pool and tennis courts while having significantly less upkeep and provided a neighborhood setting that Lori was now seeking for the kids.

We moved into our new home in September 1991 and happily remained there for the next twenty-seven years. Most of the families are still the original owners, and we have made lifelong friends. In hindsight, it was the perfect scenario for us, however it took an act of God to get us there.

The year 1991 is the same year that the great professional basketball player Earvin Magic Johnson announced that he had contracted the HIV virus. I recall the sheer horror of that announcement. For the first time in my life, this epidemic became real.

This was God's way of punishing gay men; they deserved to get this terrible deadly disease. I was terribly judgmental, cruel, and near Neanderthal in my thoughts and views on the subject of homosexuality.

What was wrong with me? What happened to my extensive Judaic-Christian-faith-based background? Wasn't I programmed to love thy neighbor as thy self and to give and share love at all costs?

I aspired to be a human being committed to making my life an example and not a warning. An individual fueled by a passion inside of me to help those who cannot help themselves.

The nineties were an absolute roller coaster for me. We were faced with a very challenging heart condition for my father-in-law, Hal.

Harold Weinberger was one of the kindest, sweetest, smartest most empathetic men I ever came to know, embrace, and love. Our relationship unfortunately lasted only a brief time, just thirteen years.

Hal Weinberger died on August 19, 1993 living a full life in the span of just sixty short years. My father-in-law was a self-made millionaire by the time he was fifty. Unfortunately his wonderful, giant heart would only last for ten more years once he achieved his financial milestone.

His thirst to live a life of passion ended thirty days after undergoing heart transplant surgery in Johns Hopkins Hospital in Baltimore, Maryland. Hal grew up in the Bronx, raised by his mother after his father passed away at a very early age. He served in the army during the Korean War as a cook, and his passion for cooking and enjoying food with friends and family never waned.

When Hal was presented with his honorable discharge from the army, he went to work to help support not only himself but his aging mother as well. Hal quickly became a successful account manager for a business machine manufacturer, which in short order paved the way for him to start his own multi-line manufacturer's representative organization covering the mid-Atlantic region of the United States.

Hal was young, aggressive, smart, and a man of faith. This combination led him to owning the rights to the entire United States for a fast-tracking office furniture manufacturer out of Canada. Coupled with the greatest stretch of postwar boom for business, Hal and his US company were flying high.

These were the Sixties and Seventies, along with his former [13]Rockette wife Dolores, they started a family and life was good. However, in the late Seventies, Hal and his partner began having differences of opinion on how to run the company. These challenges most certainly contributed to Hal's stress level, which most likely advanced his heart issues, culminating in his decision to sell his part of the business. During the negotiation process, Hal would suffer a massive heart attack that would be the beginning of the end.

In short order, Hal would go on to have a stent procedure and bypass surgery to help his ailing heart muscle. These procedures successfully prolonged his life, but the heart was too badly damaged. Ultimately he would require heart transplant surgery.

Hal had an infectious laugh. Once he started it was next to impossible to be in the same room and not join him. Hal left us way too soon; he would enjoy our son, Adam, for seven years and our daughter, Jordy, for four.

"It has been 11 months since my last journal entry. Well 1993 turned out to be a year of change. In August the family lost Hal and Grandma Travagline [my mother, Helen's mom]. Hal's loss was a monumental blow to me, Lori, Dolores and the kids. Children your grandfather was a wonderful man" (12.19.93, journal excerpt).

The 1990s were turning out to be a complete and utter emotional mess.

I was thirty-three years old, and I had lost my friend and mentor in business. It was time for me to grow up. All of a sudden, I felt I was alone, and I lost my passion for the business. I remember feeling trapped. I wanted to change careers but did not have the financial ability to sell my business or leave my current line of work.

"Hear my advice and act: Go to college then go to law, medical or business school. Become a professional first than do what you want later.

---

[13] The Rockettes (1925–modern day), the legendary Radio City Music Hall, New York City–based dance team.

Don't get trapped later in life needing greater educational skills, like me. I love you both good night" (12.19.93, end, journal excerpt).

How did this happen so quickly? Hal should have been with me for another twenty to twenty-five years advising me on my next move, but he was gone, and I was miserable.

The next several years remained much the same. I owned and operated a business I did not love in an industry that was undergoing a complete structural change. My expenses were increasing, and my income was flat.

I needed something to change, and that change would have to come by me making the conscious decision to turn inward.

1995 (Age Thirty-Five)
A Personal Journal Excerpt

Again my '95 is filled with goals and desires for growth and fulfillment. If I accomplish one thing this year, I hope it is the ability to always control my state of being. To be fully connected with the universe and to turn into a person who looks from love and service first.

My commitment is now purpose not outcome. I will continue to search for that which will allow me to propel my life to greatness. I have an intense desire to contribute to mankind in a major way. I will begin on a small level and grow into taking massive and focused action for all.

Remember what Victor Frankel said in *Man's Search for Meaning,* *"Your purpose must be greater than yourself."*

Don't just exist live with passion, excitement, and love.

When your life becomes boring and you feel you don't want to go on, change your life.

Have the courage to make the changes that make you excited to get up in the morning.

Follow your purpose, your desires, and your dreams, then life will be worth living.

Good night, and may God be with you all forever. Love, Dad.

In 1996, the kids were ten and seven, both were playing sports, my wife was working full-time in her business International Violin

Company (IVC), which we purchased in 1993 shortly after Hal's passing.

International Violin Company had been owned by just two individuals consecutively for over fifty years. My wife purchased the business from the second owner, who was in failing health and wanted the business to continue.

Located in one of the worst sections of Baltimore, International Violin Company was a sleeping giant. The business itself has a great niche and a very passionate, loyal and intense customer base. The company, still in existence today, specializes in the sale of violins, violas, cellos and bases as well as parts and accessories.

At the time of purchase, the business was being operated by three very capable young professionals, Cecilia Patterson, operations manager, and twin brothers Kenny, sales manager, and Denny Wise, service manager. They remain today, the heart and soul of the team working in conjunction with Lori.

The owner entered the hospital with her illness and never returned to the business. My wife would never have the opportunity to have her understand how to run the business as was promised.

My wife is an extraordinary person, highly intelligent, possessing a true understanding of how to operate a business. In very short order, the company added an 800 phone number and purchased a computer system that would automate the inventory and billing process.

In years to come, they would publish a color catalog, create a website capable of accepting orders, and maintain relationships with the finest manufacturers around the world. The company grew and became a leader in the industry.

My wife would go on to serve on the board and ultimately become president of the Violin Society of America (VSA).

Not bad for someone that had never played any type of musical instrument or was involved in the music business prior to becoming the owner. Can you imagine how she must have felt the first few years owning a business that was completely foreign to her?

I can, but she always had two things from day one: a burning passion to succeed and belief in her own abilities. This coupled with her new family members, Cecilia, Kenny, and Denny, became a winning formula.

In 1998, *"Coretta Scott King, widow of civil rights leader Martin Luther King, calls on the civil rights community to join the struggle against homophobia. She receives criticism from members of the black civil rights movement for comparing civil rights to gay rights"* (PBS.org).

I often think of these years (1996–2005) as the lost years. Biblically these are referred to the years that the locust have eaten (Joel 2:25). However, our God is a loving god, and he provides restoration through grace and abundance once we seek his mercy through repentance.

During this time, I traveled both domestically and internationally extensively with my business partner and friend Tony Diamante. We were building a business that would serve us both well for many years; however, I was slowly losing my soul.

I was not a very compassionate, loving, or understanding person. In retrospect, I was morphing into an uncontrollable, self-centered individual, leaving my wife at home to run a business and a household and raise the children.

I thank God each and every day that she stuck by me through this period as I am sure that she had many a night that were filled with disbelief and doubt about our future together.

I on the other hand was almost solely focused on material success. I ate poorly, exercised infrequently, drove countless miles, flew constantly and lived in and out of hotels. I had no idea who I really was and what I really wanted. All I knew that this business was my life and it became my identity.

I seemingly had everything. In reality, I had nothing. As time will reveal, the things that should have mattered most were discarded by things that mattered least.

Life on the road is what you make it. I made it more difficult than it ever had to be. This was my choice. For nearly a decade I was spiritually dead. I elected not to write in my journal, study the masters, and read the Bible, yet there was a copy in my hotel room each night.

Until the day my children elected to play youth sports, and I once again came alive. I was asked to help coach my son, Adam, in youth baseball and lacrosse; this spark rekindled my passion for life outside of work.

Adam was and still is a good athlete; however, athletics were not his passion. Adam always had an athletic build. Even as a young man he had broad shoulders, had muscular arms and legs, and was extremely fast. Adam did not share my passion for athletics. His passion came to manifest in his desire to sing and play the guitar.

I love my son, and I am so proud of his musical talent and pray that he will pursue his passion and be fortunate enough to create a good livelihood, which will also provide him with daily joy and inner peace.

In (2016) my son and the company that he is a partner received a very distinguished award for their bluegrass music event that they hold annually in Baltimore, Maryland.

In 1996, Jordy was seven, and she loved to play little league baseball on the boy's team in Pikesville, Maryland. Being one of two girls on the team did not stop Jordy from being one of the best. Jordy loved to play baseball and did so for two years until she discovered her true love, lacrosse.

I remember the day that I discovered that Jordy was destined for greatness in the sport of lacrosse. In 1997, I bought a wooden lacrosse stick; the stick itself was bigger than her. Jordy took to the stick like a duck takes to water.

Just as natural as can be, she would gently cradle the stick using her left hand as the dominate hand. When we engaged in playing catch and throw, she used her left hand flawlessly. My wife and I are both right-handed and have no one in the family that is left-handed.

Well, wait just a minute, we did have one person of influence in Jordy's life that was left-handed, and that was her stay-at-home nurse and live-in, Ms. Martha Jah. She may be the most incredible woman I have ever met outside of my wife. Martha was and is today a beautiful, strong, intelligent, and loving person. She joined our family courtesy of the rebellion that was raging in Liberia on the ivory coast of Africa.

We needed someone to help with our children since my wife and I both worked full-time in our businesses. My wife is very connected in the community, and she was able to find an agency that would provide a person to help us for a fee. Interestingly, Martha is left-handed. All through the day as she did chores around the house, she would swaddle Jordy to her back, and she became a part of her daily chores.

It is clear that Jordy mimicked Martha's use of her left hand, so when it was time for her to hold a lacrosse stick, Jordy preferred the use of her left hand as her dominant hand. Little did she know that Martha gave Jordy the greatest gift she could ever bestow upon her: the gift of being a left-handed-dominant lacrosse player.

Left-hand-dominant lacrosse players are rare. However, with Jordy's natural ability for lacrosse, her left-hand mastery, a lacrosse coach father, the perfect storm was taking place, and she would go on to take full advantage of the scenario.

Jordy's DNA would mold her into a five-foot-tall, athletic-built, quick, left-hand-dominant attacker. Being left-handed means that she would go on to feed (assist) right hand dominate midfielders cutting to the cage in their stride and strong-hand dominant, providing them with a pinpoint pass to their sticks, resulting in a career of assists, a record Jordy would go on to set at Georgetown University.

Jordy's career blossomed at the middle school level, where she would go on to lead the McDonogh Eagles in scoring and assists. While leading her teams to championships in the summer at both Lax Max (1998) and Lax Splash (2000) with her town program.

In 1999, she attended a paid clinic that would benefit the Women's National Team. Jordy was the belle of the ball; the national team players loved and embraced her as this tiny left-handed lacrosse player demonstrated her lacrosse prowess at age ten.

The movie *Austin Powers* was popular at the time, and Jordy was dubbed mini-me to one of the elite national team's player. I vividly recall walking away from that day realizing that in two cycles or in eight years, she would be eligible to play for this team.

She did and in 2007, Jordy would make the United States U19 Women's lacrosse team, earning the MVP award during the championship match versus Australia, notching one goal and five assists and leading her team to the gold medal.

Jordy would go on to complete four years of varsity play at Georgetown University. She led her team to three regular season Big East championships and one tournament championship.

On the field, she would also establish a record, which still stands today, the only player in Georgetown Women's lacrosse history to compile 100 goals and 100 assists in a career. Jordy graduated from ol' hilltop with 116 goals and 105 assists, for a total of 221 points, landing her as the number 4 all-time point leaders in Georgetown Women's Lacrosse history.

Many coaches at the NCAA Division 1 level elected not to recruit Jordy because of her height. I have spoken too many since that time, and they all to a person regret not making the conscience effort to pursue the little lefty.

All except one, Georgetown women's head lacrosse coach Ricky Fried, who, like his father before him, would elect to coach a Kirr. Unreal as it may seem, I had the distinct pleasure of playing at West Point for Ricky's dad, Coach Colonel Fried. The legacy would continue as I had played for his father, Jordy would play for Ricky (2008–2011).

To say I was happy to welcome in a new year and a new millennium is an understatement. The Nineties were a great test. They challenged every aspect of my personal being mentally, physically, emotionally, financially, spiritually, and professionally.

In many ways, I was evolving in reverse.

However, through it all, I was being blessed and being held in the palm of His hand. As I made mistake after mistake, misstep after misstep, it was he who was keeping me from total personal and professional destruction.

My God, my source, had a plan for my life and this source; this love would lead me through this trying decade.

The 90's

LGBTQ Milestones

> ➢ August 18, 1990. "President Bush signs the Ryan White care act, a federally funded program for people living with AIDS." (The [14]Ryan White Comprehensive AIDS Resources Emergency (Care) Act, Pub. L.101-381, 104 stat. 576, August 18, 1990)

> ➢ 1993. The US military enacts, "Don't Ask, Don't Tell" policy which prohibited the military from asking a service member about their sexual orientation. Prior to this groundbreaking policy gay men and lesbian women were banned from serving their country. The policy remained intact until repealed in 2011, however if service men and women were caught engaging in same sex conduct they were expelled from their branch of service. (washingtonpost.com/ Timeline: A history of Don't ask don't tell)

> ➢ 1996. The defense of marriage act is signed into law by president, Bill Clinton, a law that defined marriage as a legal union between a man and a woman and that no state is required to recognize a same-sex marriage from another state. (En.m.wikipedia.org/key words: Defense of Marriage Act)

---

[14] *Ryan White an Indiana teenager contracted AIDS in 1984 through a tainted hemophilia treatment. After being barred from school because of his HIV-positive status, Ryan became a well-known activist for AIDS research and antidiscrimination.* (Ryan White (1971-1990), ryanwhite.com)

WILLIAMSBURG

Two souls, one heart.

—French proverb

*Colonial Williamsburg is the center for history and
citizenship, encouraging national and international
audiences to learn from the past through preservation
restoration and presentation of 18th century
Williamsburg and the study, interpretation, and
teaching of America's founding democratic principles.*

That may all be well and good and it is, but from December 26 through 28, 2014, Lori, Jordy, Jaclyn, and I would spend the days enjoying Wedmore Place, the Williamsburg Winery, the Fat Canary, and of course taking in the sights and sounds of colonial Williamsburg.

Opened in 1983, the Wedmore Inn sits on land that was first tilled as a farm in 1615. However, it was not until 1985 that the first grapes were planted on the land. The hotel, the Wedmore Inn, and the Williamsburg Winery (WW) sit nestled on three hundred acres of beautiful Virginia land.

The European-style country hotel boasts twenty-eight stunning rooms, all of which include a delicious continental breakfast that is served in the "buttery" each morning.

Like all guests at Wedmore, we were treated to a complimentary tour and wine tasting at the Williamsburg Winery. While at Wedmore, we also were able to enjoy sitting by a roaring fire in a colonial decorated den, lounging by the pool, albeit empty, and enjoying dinner at Café Provencal, which serves up masterful French cuisine.

The trip was our gift to the girls in celebration of their engagement earlier in the month. Jordy and Jaclyn were engaged on a cold Friday evening December 12, 2014, in Iowa City, Iowa.

Jaclyn was the assistant women's volleyball coach at the University of Iowa. The moment was all planned out by Jaclyn, but Jordy's rambunctious nature derailed the gazebo setting in the downtown square, and they ended up exchanging their love for each other in the car.

Love has a way of transcending all other circumstances; it would be the case on this monumental evening as well.

Prior to the trip to Williamsburg, Lori and I hosted an engagement party at the house earlier in the week. As luck would have it, we had excellent weather, which precipitated a very large turnout of friends and family, all except the grandfathers (Jaclyn's mother's father and my father).

We were very concerned about how both would take the news that their granddaughters were gay and were engaged to be married. Looking back, it is hard to believe that we kept the news of Jordy's sexual orientation a secret from her grandfather for what was now the better part of three years.

These are men that grew up in a time when being gay was not only looked down upon in society but was seen as immoral and criminal in nature. We knew that ultimately we were going to have to tell both of them unless they would go to be with the Lord before being pressed to tell them of the news. As it turned out, both were alive and both would have to be told, but the person, time, and place had to be measured to achieve the best result.

December 26 was a beautiful day for our 195 mile journey that with coffee breaks normally takes on an average of about 4 hours. As you can imagine, the day after Christmas is a massive travel day, as friends and family bid a fond adieu to their love ones and begin their travels back to their homes, some having to get back to work while others would begin preparing for the New Year celebrations.

Our 4-hour drive became 5-plus, but we arrived in time to enjoy the final afternoon wine tasting tour.

The Williamsburg Winery is a unique vineyard reminiscent of the timeless traditions of eighteenth-century winemaking. You will enjoy award-winning vintages prepared in the classic European style, albeit with assistance from modern technology to perfect the quality.

In recent years, the winery has received awards at the decanter world wine competition in the UK.

Before Patrick Duffeler, the Belgium-born businessman came to Virginia to open a winery and boutique hotel, he held executive positions with Phillip Morris and other companies in Europe. Duffeler purchased the 320-acre Wessex hundred farm in James City County in 1983 and planted his first crop in '85.

The first wine produced in 1988, Governor's White, won the Williamsburg Winery its first award, a gold medal from the Virginia governor's cup, just two weeks after its introduction. It remains the winery's most popular wine to this day.

Production has increased from 2,500 cases 20 years ago to more than 65,000 cases today. The winery's 50-plus acres of vineyards produce six grape varieties, including Petite Verdot, Merlot, and Cabernet Franc. Duffeler employs up to 70 people during the peak season, June through October.

Since its inception, the winery has received more than 250 awards. Its Acte 12 Chardonnay was rated "One of the best wines in the world" by Decanter Magazine in 2007 and 2008.

Our tasting and tour guide was a retired professional who loved his job more than anyone I had ever had the pleasure of knowing. Well, in retrospect, who would not love showing folks around a beautiful winery in a country setting, sipping, sharing, and extoling the virtues of the different wines.

Slowly we became enthralled with the beauty of the day, the cadence of our guide's storytelling, the suppleness of the wine, and one another's company. We were bonding, delighting in one another's happiness and our shared joy for this newfound relationship.

When the tour ended, I purchased a half-dozen bottles of our favorite wine, and we headed back across the compound to the Wedmore Inn. Our spirits were high, and we all wanted to keep the glow ablaze, so we uncorked a bottle and headed to a cozy den just off the lobby. The den was decorated in eighteenth-century furniture and configured for conversation.

We playfully poked and pried one another as to our likes and dislikes, attempting to uncover some shred of information that we had not yet discovered about one another. The wine flowed, and the time passed quickly as we realized that we needed to get ready for our dinner at one of our favorite restaurants in Williamsburg, the Fat Canary.

"When the ships sailed from the Old World to the New, they stopped in the Canary Islands for supplies. One of the most important provisions brought aboard was wine, referred to Canary" (fatcanarywilliamsburg. com).

The restaurant is named after a reference in the Colonial-era playwright, John Lyly's poem: *"Oh for a bowl of fat canary, rich Palermo, sparkling sherry"* (John Lyly).

Located in the heart of Colonial Williamsburg, the Fat Canary has received the AAA four diamond awards for each of the past ten years.

Our daytime December heat wave (sixty-ish) gave way to the hawk and more typical winter temperatures. I recall how beautiful all the ladies looked that evening. I was the luckiest man alive to be surrounded by the company of babes.

It was a Friday evening during one of Colonial Williamsburg's busiest seasons. The entire city was radiant glowing from the white lights, candles and sparkling ornaments from the many Christmas trees in the main square.

We were alive, we were in love, and we were hungry. Jordy and Jaclyn enjoy and appreciate fine dining, and Lori and I were excited to share this restaurant and evening with them.

Our waitress was our age. I could tell that she needed some time to adjust to this party of four, but I must admit she did pivot quickly and was a joy throughout the evening. Our table was in the back of the restaurant but faced the open kitchen. The ladies loved being able to watch all the great dishes being prepared. I could not have handpicked a more appropriate table for our dining experience.

We openly shared our special occasion with the waitress, and she responded by bringing us champagne on the house for our toast. The night was just getting better and better.

Maine Lobster, Rappahannock Oysters, and ginger barbecued ribs were a masterful start, and we were just hitting our stride.

Our Virginia Viognier was superb, inciting abundant laughter as our engagement dinner celebration was in full swing.

King Salmon, Seared Sea Scallops, Pan Roasted Duck, and Prime Beef Tenderloin were each served to our personal preference. All of sudden, there was silence as no one had the desire or ability to speak as we smiled, nodded, and used hand gestures to convey our delight.

We did not want this night to end. It was magical, it was wonderful, and it was ours forever. Taking our cue, the waitress had the restaurant prepare a wonderful dessert once again in honor of their engagement. We kept the evening alive with coffee and after drink cordials. Finally we had come to the end. There was nothing left to order.

As we departed, we were escorted by staff and adoring patrons, who seemed eager to offer their congratulations to the now-famous couple.

Camelot was alive and well, and it acted out in splendid array at the Fat Canary.

The morning of December 27 greeted us with brilliant sunshine. Little did we know that we would enjoy a day time temperatures that would soar into the low seventies. Upon waking we enjoyed a leisurely cup of coffee in our classically appointed French-influenced Gascony room.

As previously mentioned each room at Wedmore is unique and styled after a region in Europe.

Our Gascony room was inspired by region located in an area of Southwest France. *"Gascony is famed for the 'douceur de vivre' (sweetness of life), its food (home of foie gras) and Armagnac (brandy) its medieval towns and villages locally called 'bastides.' These villages are nestled amidst green rolling hills, sunny weather, beautiful landscapes and an occasional view of the 'Pyrannes' mountain range"* (About- France.com).

The ladies on the other hand were enjoying the Languedoc room, paying homage to a historical coastal region in Southern France. The region is dominated by 740,300 acres of vineyards, a Mediterranean climate, and plenty of land with the soil being extremely suitable for the production of wine.

We made plans the evening before to meet in the buttery for breakfast, where we would luxuriate in our warmly ensconced sur-

rounding while feasting on a lavish selection of meats, cheeses, crois-
sants, juices, and French-pressed coffee. What a wonderful start to an
even more wonderful day.

We decided to use this day to enjoy all that Colonial Williamsburg
had to offer. Dressed for December, we all began peeling off the lay-
ers of clothes we wore by midmorning.

Our first stop for the day would be the Governor's Palace.

The tour through the Governor's Palace was remarkable, due
to the fact that we arrived early there was no line and our tour guide
was excellent. What I did notice was that a few of the older folks in
our tour group could not stop watching Jordy and Jaclyn as they held
hands and openly expressed their affection for each other.

How ironic that in a building celebrating the lifestyle of the
political leaders of the state of Virginia, two women of the same sex
would be permitted to freely share their love for each other.

A 1975 statute prohibited Virginia from recognizing same
sex marriage for nearly forty years. However, on October 6, 2014,
following a decision by the Supreme Court of the United States to
refuse to hear an appeal of the fourth Circuit Court of Appeals in the
case of *Bostic v. Schaefer.*

Virginia along with thirty-six other states preceded the Supreme
Court's decision on June 25, 2015, to provide same-sex couples the
right to marry in all fifty states. The 5–4 decision prohibited states from
not allowing a couple to marry and must legally recognize their unions.

Hence just several months after Virginia's landmark decision,
the older generation on our tour would quietly voice their disap-
proval by their whispers, pointing, and facial expressions, which publicly demonstrated their disdain.

As we strolled down dirt paths and over grass-covered courts,
the sunshine was our constant companion as were the stares, the
pointing, and the looks of disgust on many of the older and conservative men and women who had ascended on Colonial Williamsburg
on this day just two days removed from the celebration of the birth
of Jesus Christ.

This town is steep in tradition, conservatism, and America's
Christian values. It is clear that many of the folks that come to

Williamsburg from all over the country do so to reinforce their love and passion for like-minded morals and values.

The good news is that the ladies seemed oblivious to it all. Throughout the day, at lunch, in and out of shops and must-see places of interest, they enjoyed the day in a rapture of hand-holding, cuddles, and soft kisses.

Mother and I loved being with them. We were not uncomfortable in the least bit. We knew the depth of their love, and no one was going to make us feel any different. We refused to give these folks permission to make us feel any different than we did.

Elated that our daughter had found the love of her life and delighted to have Jaclyn as part of our family!

As the late afternoon settled in, we decided that it was time to enjoy the balance of the day relaxing with a bottle of wine and easing into our dinner plans at Wedmore.

Upon returning, we headed out to the poolside area of the hotel, but the December air convinced us to return to the first-floor study off the lobby, where we enjoyed the warmth of the roaring fire created by the hotel staff.

Sprawled on the tufted sofas we enjoyed a perfect interlude to the perfect day.

Café Provencal is located in the rear of the main floor of the Wedmore Inn with expansive windows overlooking a beautifully landscaped courtyard.

The decoration is pure Provence. The walls are adorned with French country utensils and tasteful artwork, which serve to transport you to a roadside inn somewhere adjacent to rolling vineyards and roaming livestock.

The tables and chairs are rustic but very comfortable. White and royal blue are the consistent colors of tablecloths, seat cushions, and drapery. It is impossible not to be consumed by the warm, inviting feeling that the restaurant and staff provide.

Being foodies, the ladies were extremely excited for the gastronomical extravaganza that awaited us all. We began the meal appropriately so, choosing another great bottle of the Winery's finest.

Our toast was radiant complete with the ladies, thanking Mother and I for the trip, and the chance to get away for a few days and enjoy each other as a newly engaged couple.

As a prelude, we began with butternut squash soup and a butcher board complete with a variety of delicacies that primed our palettes for the main course.

In the spirit of the French culture, we enjoyed choosing dishes that were a natural match, including seared duck breast and lamb. Our diner was wonderful, the conversation lively and dripping with gratitude.

Of course we enjoyed *la douceur de vivre* (the sweetness of life) with a wonderful assortment of homemade cookies and decaf coffee. Our eyes were giving way. Our day was rapidly coming to an end. We all walked back together to our rooms, said our good-nights, and slipped into the comfort of our beautiful abode.

Bonne nuit!

Sunday was a bit more brisk than the past several days, and our car was covered in a light layer of early-morning frost. I was set forth by the ladies to gather up the car and prepare the cabin for our journey home.

Gladly I accepted the opportunity to check us out of the inn, load our luggage into the trunk, and ready our vehicle for the four-plus-hour journey back to Baltimore.

Basking in the glow of a fabulous weekend, I collected the ladies who were still saying their final goodbyes to the very friendly and attentive staff inside the cavernous lobby adorned in all her traditional Christmas gala.

As we made our way down the long driveway, we all sensed that something magical had occurred and that this weekend would be our memory forever.

The love that was shared by Jordy and Jaclyn this weekend was transformational, and in an instant, I wanted to find a way to help others navigate their journey, as I had mine.

Our light banter turned to Jaclyn's upcoming interview for the women's head volleyball coaching position at George Mason University in Fairfax, Virginia. Jaclyn had briefed us on the exciting news before our trip, but now she was enquiring if we could make a detour home and check out the campus and the facilities.

Without hesitation, I bellowed with excitement that we would love to visit the campus on the way home and offered to stop for a bite to eat before the final leg of our trip back home.

Like our trip to Williamsburg, the return was not much better as we fought our way along 95 North entangled with families returning home from their Christmas visits to Aunt Edna and Uncle Ralph.

George Mason is a sprawling campus just on the fringe of the city of Fairfax. Mason is the largest public research University in Virginia, with over 100 million dollars invested in research in 2015. It is the home to 34,000 students hailing from 130 countries.

Jaclyn had just completed her season as the assistant coach at the up and coming Iowa Hawkeyes in the Big Ten. Jaclyn's résumé was impressive, and her confidence level was high. We all agreed that this would be a wonderful place to begin her head coaching career.

We merrily snaked our away through and around the desolate campus as all the students were home and enjoying a month-long repose from the academic grind of a college semester. As we exited the back end of Mason, we all agreed that we had seen enough and it was time to grab some a late lunch early dinner before completing the final ninety-minute drive back home.

Having been to Fairfax many times for business, I knew a place that I wanted to share with the ladies, the Hard Times Café, serving several different types chili over pasta, with a cornucopia of fresh toppings and ice-cold beer. Now who could argue with that invitation? No one did, just as I had hoped.

No sooner had we arrived at the table, Lori's phone rang. It was my sister, Renee. Since my mom passed away, Renee and I have alternated spending either Saturday or Sunday with my father, who was eighty-three years old at the time.

The entire family was aware that Jordy was gay and now engaged to Jaclyn, all but one—my dad. As mentioned, we were highly concerned how my father would accept the news that his only granddaughter was gay and was engaged to be married to another woman.

The plan was for Jordy and Jaclyn to meet with my father and break the news to him in person without a lot of others around. That plan would never unfold.

Renee told us over the phone that my father now knew that Jordy was gay and would be wed to Jaclyn in due time. But how and why did this occur?

Well, here goes, my sister, my nephew, JR, and his girlfriend, Becca, all had finished having dinner at a restaurant near our house when they decided to bring Dad back to watch the Baltimore Ravens football team play.

Unbeknownst to them, they did not realize that we had not completed cleaning up from our engagement party the night before we left for our trip. There were multiple signs throughout the house congratulating Jordy and Jackie on their engagement.

As my father entered the house, he was immediately greeted with a big heart that read "Jordy loves Jackie!" Turning to my sister, my father asked who was Jackie and why he was not informed of the engagement.

Realizing they had made a huge mistake bringing my father back to the house, they had no choice but to face the music. Becca informed my father that Jackie was Jordy's girlfriend and now wife to be.

Upon hearing that Jackie was a woman, Renee and company strangely sensed my father was relieved, but for what reason? After additional conversation, my father, challenged by racial equality, tied the name Jackie to a man, and the only man that my father knew named Jackie was the famous African American baseball legend Jackie Robinson.

Welcome to 2014, when someone is relieved that their loved one is gay versus married to a person of color. When we arrived home, everyone was waiting for us, and my father embraced Jordy and Jaclyn and their union.

I am proud of my father. He has been kind, loving, and supportive from day one. We should have told him the truth from the start!

New Millennium

What we do in life echoes in eternity.

— The Movie *Gladiator*, 2000

The limousine quietly pulled up and settled in my driveway. It was sleek, a brand-new Lincoln with room for ten. My wife coaxed me outside, and I immediately knew what was happening, she had done it again, it was part of my surprise fortieth birthday party.

Unlike the pizza party we enjoyed for my thirtieth, this was going to be some weekend. As Lori and I entered the limo, we were greeted by four other couples and our destination was Atlantic City (AC), New Jersey.

Living in Baltimore during this time, it was practically customary to head to AC for the weekend for a little gambling, great restaurants, nightlife, and the beach. These were the hey days of AC before gambling was legalized in the state of Maryland.

Many of us not being big gamblers were going to enjoy my birthday party at the Trump Taj Mahal, spend a night away from the kids, and enjoy one another's friendship. My lovely wife had once again given me a gift of a lifetime, one that I still cherish to this day.

During the ten years that led up to this party, my mother-in-law, Dolores, and my father-in-law, Hal, were extremely good customers at this hotel and casino. The Taj Mahal Hotel and Casino opened its doors on April 2, 1990, and was a huge success from day one. It was complete with 167,000 square feet of gaming space, 2,010 hotel rooms and multiple 4-star restaurants.

The casino was developed by Donald Trump at a cost of nearly one billion dollars. My party was held at my favorite restaurant and premier steakhouse, Safari.

No expense was spared for our guests during our stay, and the birthday celebration was fabulous. I remember feeling as though I was on top of the world. I recall mentioning to my wife that I would love to have a Rolex watch as a gift to commemorate this milestone birthday. I never said another word, until I was presented with my gift at the party. It has adorned my wrist every day since as constant reminder to always pursue excellence.

Surrounded by friends and family, I turned forty years old with a great wife, two healthy children, a partner in a promising business venture, and the love of both my mother and father.

Little did I know that over the course of the next two years, some of these circumstances would change forever, and they would set in motion a change of events that would inexorably alter the course of my entire future.

However, for one bright and shining weekend, I was on top of the world. I had survived the tumultuous nineties, and for the first time in a long time, my life was trending in a very positive fashion.

Shortly after returning home from my dream like weekend, I began to notice some changes in my health. I was constantly thirsty, urinating frequently, and began to suffer from blurred vision. However, I shrugged off these symptoms and chalked it up to turning forty.

Until one evening, when under the watchful eye of a physician, who happened to be sitting at the same table as I at a wedding reception, asked me if I had a drug problem. The doctor was a friend of mine, and he asked me alone and in strict confidence. My answer was an emotional no, backed by, "Why do you ask such a question?"

His words still affect me today. He respectfully said, "I have noticed you are constantly running to the bathroom, and you seem to be drinking an inordinate amount of water. I told him that I did recently notice this but dismissed it as signs of getting older."

That is when he said those fate-filled words, "Have you ever been tested for diabetes?"

"No," I replied, "but will be sure to have my doctor run a test during my next physical."

"No, you don't understand," he shot back. "You need to address this immediately. Tonight if at all possible."

The next morning would bring much of the same symptoms, so I told my wife that I was going to the local Patient First office to get checked, as per the doctor's recommendation. About an hour later,

I was told by the attending physician at Patient First that my blood sugar level was over 800 mg/dl and I should have been in a diabetic coma or dead.

For those of you that are unfamiliar with blood sugar levels, a normal healthy person has a blood sugar level of between 80–100 mg/dl. I drove myself to the medical facility with a level 8x the norm, accompanied by an A1C level of 17 percent, again a normal and healthy person has an A1C level between 6 and 7 percent.

A1C is a blood test that shows the average amount of sugar (glucose) in your blood over the past 2 to 3 months. Overnight my life was altered forever; I would now have to dedicate myself to eating a healthy diet, daily exercise, and medication to control this deadly disease that I had inherited from my family bloodline.

Tuesday, September 11, 2001, was a spectacular day throughout the eastern portion of the United States. A high pressure system perfectly positioned delivered bright sunshine and temperatures in the low seventies.

As I traveled down Rockville Pike, a main artery in a suburb of our nation's capital, I received a call at 9:00 a.m. from my business partner in northern New Jersey. He asked me where I was and had I heard the news. I informed him that I was near Washington, DC, on appointments and wasn't listening to the news.

Our business was in located in Clifton, New Jersey, a small blue-collar town with areas zoned for business used primarily by small- to medium-size light manufacturing or distribution companies. We were engaged in a little of both, as a pick and pack entity and a light manufacturer of custom office furniture.

My partner Tony was an amicable and extremely hard working professional, and in the fifteen-plus years we had worked together, I never heard him this concerned about any issue. Oh, yes, there was the one time when I did make the mistake of calling him at home during his dinner, a sacred time for many Italian Americans.

He informed me that a plane, American Airlines Flight 11, had crashed into the North Tower of the World Trade Center in downtown Manhattan between floors 93–99 at 8:46 a.m., killing everyone on board.

Twenty minutes later, at 9:03 a.m., Tony informed me that United Airlines Flight 175 hit the South Tower between floors 75–85. This was an act of planned terror against the United States of America.

In the interim, I had turned on the news and was following the day's events via the radio and going about my day conducting business in the area. At each appointment, the business owner was completely absorbed by the news in New York, making it next to impossible to conduct business as usual.

At 9:37 a.m., hijackers aboard flight 77 crash into the western façade of the Pentagon in Washington, DC, killing 59 aboard the plane and 125 military and civilian inside the building.

After just one hour from the first plane striking the North Tower, the FAA ordered all civilian flights over the United States airspace grounded. The news bureaus were now warning all US citizens of potential attacks in key cities and landmarks around the country, especially the home of our president and the cradle of American democracy, Washington, DC.

Realizing my proximity to DC and that today was going to be a difficult day to do business, I headed for home just before 11:00 a.m. The drive to Baltimore on a regular weekday takes about 45 minutes. However, this was no normal day. I arrived home to my beloved at just past 3:00 p.m.

During my trip home, both towers collapsed, lower Manhattan south of Canal Street was evacuated, and all schools and businesses were being told to close. Everyone was instructed to go home and stay at home. This caused a mass and frenzied exodus. America was under attack, and we had no clue how to handle this situation.

Little did I realize the effect that this day's events would have on me personally as the days, weeks, and months ahead brought commerce in the New York metropolitan area to a grinding halt. As a distribution company that depended on the New York piers to receive, inspect and move 40 feet containers in 3–5 days from receipt. Overnight, the process went from days to weeks.

Business slowed, billing weakened, and our cash reserve dwindled before our eyes. We quickly knew we were in trouble.

The phone was ringing off the hook as I entered my office from a late lunch appointment on October 30, 2001. It was my mother, and it also happened to be her 66th birthday. There were 2 things wrong with this scenario: my mother never called me at the office and she never called me during the business day.

I quickly assumed she wanted to give me a hard time for not yet calling and wishing her a happy birthday, which I was just about to do before she called me.

After singing happy birthday to her, she quietly said, "Thank you, but I have something to tell you." I had my annual physical last week, and they did their routine battery of tests. Normally they call me and let me know all is well and they will see me next year. This time that wouldn't be the case.

Mom was asked to set up another visit for a consultation; it was on her birthday she would find out that she had stage 4 pancreatic cancer and was given no more than six months to live.

We spoke for over an hour, as I questioned her like a detective interrogates a suspect, looking for any clue that would lead me to believe that she would be okay, perhaps with some magical combination of radiation, chemotherapy, some new age drugs, and a better diet and exercise program.

Apparently my mother must have implored the same line of questioning and probing with her doctor as she was able to deflect every ray of hope that I could muster. Yes, she would immediately begin a regiment of toxic treatment in an effort to extend her time here on earth.

By mid-December, Mom demonstrated to her caregivers that she was rapidly losing her fight. She was transferred to Gilchrist Hospice in Towson, Maryland. This would be her final stop along the way.

My mother, Helen Geraldine Kirr, lost her fight to cancer on January 17, 2002.

This day would also mark the physical and mental decline of my father William. After forty-five-plus years of marriage, my father would now be on his own to live out the remaining days without his life partner.

As promising as the new millennium started, it quickly took a turn for the worst. In just fifteen short months from my birthday, I would contract type 2 diabetes, my business would be irrevocably damaged, and I would lose my mother to cancer.

My personal faith was shaken to the core; I disconnected myself from source and was determined to fix my life on my own. Wow, what a mistake.

These were the years that the locust had eaten.

I don't know exactly when I stopped wanting to be connected to my source, but it was the beginning of many long years of doubt, fear, indecision, and wrong decision-making.

Even though I had abandoned him, he did not forsake me. My wife's business continued to do well. My children were healthy and doing well in school and enjoying their lives. In retrospect, I am so grateful that our source kept my family in the palm of his hand while he allowed me to twist and turn allowing my hubris to lead a life that was meant to be directed by him.

If I only would have allowed Proverbs 3:5–6 to work for me daily, I wonder how differently my life would be today: *"Trust in the Lord with all your heart, and lean not on your own understanding, acknowledge him in all your ways and he will make your paths straight"* (Holy Bible, NIV).

The sages would argue that this was my dharma; it was what I had to go through in my life to get me to where I am today. If that is true, then I am grateful for God's grace and mercy for bringing me through these times and providing me with divine intelligence to make the proper changes to my life.

January 24, 2005

My first journal entries since January 16, 1997. I once again begin drafting journal entries on a semiregular basis.

> *A lot has happened since I began journaling on March 4, 1992. My message today is no different than it was thirteen years ago: follow your heart, and you will have a life filled with magic and joy.*

Do not settle. Choose your life's path, and do it with love and trust.

January 26, 2005

Children, the years go by very quickly. Enjoy the moments that are special. They will bring you comfort in your older days. A great entertainer died today, Johnny Carson, the great host of the Tonight Show, *a position he enjoyed for more than thirty years. Johnny leaves a great legacy, one filled with many memorable moments on TV. Johnny came into our homes almost every night. He made us laugh, and he built a great number of lasting friendships. Every person who watched him on a regular basis felt they knew him.*

My desire is to be remembered as someone who cared, someone who made a difference here on this earth. I hope I have made a positive impression on all of you. It has always been my intent to leave you with five things:

1. *Good name*

2. *Great education*

3. *Wonderful memories*

4. *Financial favor*

5. *Freedom to live the life you have imagined*

January 27, 2005

The secret of happiness is simple: find out what you love to do and then direct all your energy towards doing it.

February 7, 2005

I would like to create a lifestyle centered on special places and special moments. All things that are good and right can be obtained through love of all mankind and selfless service to all.

FATHER 4 THE BRIDEZ

Go forth and love and serve God and your fellow man. If you do these two simple things, your lives will be completely fulfilled.

Love Dad

As we departed the Fort Lauderdale airport, the Florida sun immediately greeted us, and we smiled gently. It was February 17, 2005, and the escape from the Baltimore winter was welcomed.

We were here on vacation, sort of. We were here to celebrate the life of a beautiful, courageous woman who happened to be one our best friends. She was dying of cancer.

Eight of us made the four-day trip, an experience that touched my heart and mind for the remainder of my life. Here was a magnificent woman, endowed with intelligence, physical prowess, and vigor for all that life had to offer.

She was forty-nine years old, had three wonderful children (triplets)—two boys and one girl—and an adoring husband. How on God's green earth could this be happening? The cancer began in her colon and by now had spread to both the liver and the lungs. On February 25, she was set to undergo a new surgical technique that would either prolong her life or shorten it drastically.

We all knew the gravity of these four days, and I am proud to say that we shared, we sang, we danced, we wined, we dined, we played, we laughed, we cried, we embraced, and we sucked the marrow from the bone of life.

I don't recall ever experiencing feeling as alive as I did from February 17–21, 2005. So what was so exhilarating? I believe that being in the presence of someone that you deeply care for and love so much and to know that each moment will be a memory in the very near future provides the impetus for this tremendous appreciation for life.

We were of different nationalities, different faiths, different income brackets. Everything about all eight of us was different, all except one unifying thread—we all loved one another, and we wanted to make these four days the very best they could be and they were.

Ten months later, our friend would pass away. This experience reaffirmed to us very valuable lessons, which each of us have heard many times before throughout our lives: to treasure each day and to love everyone more deeply.

Her passing in December 2005 caused me to examine every aspect of my life, what I discovered was a life devoid of meaning.

What was I to do? How could I possibly course correct at age 45?

December 2005

> *Dying is just the final phase of the physical world. I believe that our soul lives on forever and that one day our souls will meet again.*
> *Do not fear death, my children. Embrace life.*

My introspection centered around four questions posed by Pastor Rick Warren

1. Whom will I choose to place at the center of my life?

2. What will be the contribution of my life?

3. What will be the character of my life?

4. What will be the community of my life?

If you truly wish to discover who/what you find to be the most important force in your life. Ask yourself the above four questions if you dare.

If you're like most people, you won't. Why? Because you either will not be able to answer the questions or you will not like the answers.

Turning inward is extremely difficult. It is the hardest direction to turn as the only person that exist there is you. No one else is there to blame, no one else can answer the questions, and no one else can provide the answers.

I answered the questions in January 2006 in the following manner:

Q. Whom will I choose to place at the center of my life?
A. GOD

Q. What will be the contribution of my life?

A. Provide a godlike example through my words and actions. I feel that God wants to use me to help younger people unable to help themselves.

Q. What will be the character of my life?

A. Give, serve, love, praise, and have compassion and gratitude.

Q. What will be the community of my life?

A. God, family, friends, young adults on the street, and those that are unable to care for themselves and their children.

What are so remarkable about the answers that I recorded in my diary over ten years ago is that I would pen the same answers today. What is even more incredible is that it has taken me another decade to truly internalize my answers and convictions and to live each day with them close to my heart and mind.

Like many people in this world, I had to come to the point where I no longer wanted to disappoint my source any longer. I read all the books, I listened to all the tapes, I attended the seminars, yet I knew better than all the great sages and source how to live my life.

It wasn't till one day when I realized that I could no longer do this by myself. Yes, I had my wife now of twenty-plus years, two grown-up children, my own business, and an emptiness the size of the Grand Canyon.

I had it all, but I had nothing. My narcissism was debilitating until I humbled myself before source (God) and asked Him to fill me with humbleness, humility, gratitude, and divine intelligence.

In 2008, my partner and I sold our business, our son, Adam, graduated from Gettysburg College, Jordy finished her freshman year at Georgetown; and I turned a page, or so I thought.

It was time to walk the talk and to live each day in the service of others, while once again making God (source) the central part of my life.

Over the course of the next eight years, I would learn to once again place God squarely in the center of my universe. Live in an attitude of gratitude and happily render service to my family, friends, and fellow man with humbleness and humility.

My journey is just beginning. Yes, I am now fifty-seven years old, but I truly believe that the best days and years are ahead of me. I look forward to traveling the world and talking to folks of every walk in life.

My message is simple: we are here not to judge, but to love.

In a world where the news is dominated by terrorism, hate crimes, and discrimination by race, faith, and sexual preference, it is my hope that we will move from hate to love, from segmentation to inclusion, and parents of children that are lesbian, gay, bisexual, transgender and questioning will make the evolution from embarrassment to embracement.

Namaste

I honor the place in you in which the entire universe dwells.

I honor the place in you which is of love, light, peace and joy.

When you are in that place in you and I am in that place in me,

We Are One.
(Namaste holistic healing & yoga center, namastetruckee.com)

New Millennium

LGBTQ Milestones

> 2000. Vermont becomes the first state to legally recognize civil unions between gay or lesbian couples. The law states that these couples would be entitled to the same benefits, privileges and responsibilities as spouses. (Infoplease.com)

> 2003. The U.S. Supreme Court rules in Lawrence v. Texas that sodomy laws in the U.S. are unconstitutional. Justice Anthony Kennedy wrote, "Liberty presumes an autonomy of self that includes freedom of thought, belief, expression, and certain intimate conduct."

  In November, the Massachusetts Supreme Judicial Court ruled that barring gays and lesbians from marrying violates the state constitution.

  The Massachusetts Chief Justice concluded that to "deny the protections, benefits, and obligations conferred by civil marriage" to gay couples was unconstitutional because it denied "the dignity and equality of all individuals" and made them "second-class citizens." Strong opposition followed the ruling.' (Infoplease.com)

> 2003 Saw the first ever gay pride parade in a Muslim Country, Istanbul, Turkey (21st Century, timeline: gay and lesbian milestones)

> 2005. The Roman Catholic Church issues an instruction prohibiting any individuals who "present deep-seated homosexual tendencies or support the so called gay culture" from joining the priesthood." (Catholic.com/Homosexuality)

> In 2006 Kim Coco Iwamoto became the first transgender official to win statewide office in Hawaii. (Associated press, November 16, 2006. Hawaiian becomes highest elected transgender official.)

- ➢ 2011. End to the ban on openly gay,lesbian and bisexual people in the military (the repeal of Don't Ask, Don't Tell). (en.m.wikipedia/timeline : gay &lesbian milestones)

- ➢ 2015. The United States Supreme Court ruled in Obergefell v. Hodges that state-level bans on same sex marriage were unconstitutional. This marked the first time in history that same sex marriage was legal in all U.S. Jurisdictions. (en.m.wikipedia /timeline : gay &lesbian milestones)

Mrs. & Mrs.

*"Marriage requires falling in love many
times, always with the same person."*

—Mignon McLaughlin, American Writer

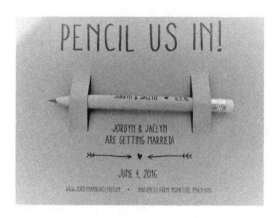

During the month of May 2016, we experienced an all-time weather anomaly. It rained seventeen straight days in a row. Now, if you lived in Seattle or London, that is no great feat, but for Baltimore, Maryland, in the month of May, this was quite disturbing.

We chose June 4, 2016, one and a half years prior to the wedding day. The girls are both a slave to an academic and athletic schedule, Jordy busy with lacrosse from January to May, and Jaclyn tied up with volleyball from August to November.

So as the fateful day approached, we all became well versed in the many facets of meteorology. We studied weather maps and charts, beginning first with the farmer's almanac, which predicted severe thunderstorms, high wind gusts, and unseasonably cool temperatures. So with this lovely forecast, we became hopelessly tethered to multiple online weather stations, each predicting a different forecast complete with high and low pressure readings, barometric pressure data, and Doppler radar.

I am sure by now that you have figured out that we had rolled the dice and elected an outdoor venue to host the big day. Apparently for many years, Jordy dreamed of having her wedding ceremony and celebration in a barn. Growing up in the suburbs of Baltimore and choosing to attend two urban universities (Georgetown and Marquette), I have no idea where she came up with the idea of a rural setting.

When I first heard the idea of a barn wedding, I envisioned guests dressed in blue jean overalls draped over white t-shirts, accompanied by straw hats and cowboy boots. The barn appropriately filled with horses, cows, pigs, and chickens. A massive wooden structure weathered and barely standing with hay floors, ceilings that revealed the summer sky, and barn doors that were unusable and unwieldy.

My vision included a justice of the peace: elderly, bespectacled, and stodgy. The music would come from a rented pipe organ, played by the lady at the local church, while the smell of manure filled the frayed nostrils of the dozen or so guests that would brave the surroundings to attend.

Horse carriers, ATVs, tractors, and plows would line the backdrop as the farm hands, and God would serve as our witness for these nuptials.

Hold that thought.

The final month leading up to the wedding day was sheer madness. My lovely and overcaring wife, Lori, slept an average of three to four hours per night and never in bed. Lori lives to please other people; she went over the details tirelessly to be sure that neither she nor any of the vendors had missed a thing.

Compounding the situation was the fact that we were having two hundred guests at a facility that if we experienced inclement weather, we would need a plan B—and, in my wife's case, a plan C as well. Little did Lori know that I had been consistently faithful and vigilant in my prayers and dialogue with our source. I knew in my heart we were going to be just fine.

My wife was absolutely incredible and deserves much of the credit for working closely with Jordy and Jaclyn and the wedding planner to create a first-class affair. Our wedding planner was lovely and played the role of referee and coordinator beautifully, pulling off an affair with many moving parts on multiple levels.

It was the end of December 2014, a cold but sunny day, as Lori, Jordy, Jaclyn, and myself headed out to see a barn on a private estate that we had heard was available, but only with permission by the owners. We had arranged an appointment with the owner's son through the friend of a friend. We had no idea what to expect. We only had one thing in mind, and we needed a barn to host a wedding.

Waiting to meet us this day was the son of the estate's owners, an affable young man, who, come to find out, actually knew some of Jordy's good friends. A bond was formed, and the ice was broken.

The estate and the grounds were magnificent. A tree-lined path escorted us onto the property and ushered us from the main house, past the twelve-stall stable on the left and to the bright-yellow barn at the bottom of the hill on the right and adjacent to a bucolic pasture adorned with show quality horses.

The main house, the owner's private residence, is something preserved from years gone by when rolling farms and plantations dotted the Maryland landscape. This wonderful masterpiece is symmetrical in every detail and radiates a patina of wealth and influence but in a warm and appealing hue.

The family that owns this property is humble and down-to-earth and completely understands the gravity of their responsibility to be good stewards of such a gift from God. For this family to share their property is a blessing on all who are fortunate enough to experience.

Shortly after we arrived, we met the mom, and she began to describe what we could expect on the first weekend of June, if all went well. She painted a lovely picture of where the ceremony could take place, directly in front of the stable, adorned with massive red roses and lush shrubs and other flowers accompanying. A massive double-trunked tree perfectly centered would mark the location for the bride and bide to take their vows.

We even discussed having all the horses present in the stable and peering out onto the wedding party. We ultimately decided against that choice as the horses can at times become noisy and unruly and we did not want to chance disturbing the ceremony in any fashion.

Even on a cold day in December, the barn itself was magnificent. It is a three-story structure, with the lower level complete with bathrooms, a refrigerator, a large antique printing press that doubles as a bar during a cocktail hour, and a beautiful stamped concrete patio that can easily hold several hundred people mixing and mingling at high-top tables.

The main floor is the same level as the lawn and stable. It is here that the band, the dance floor, the bar, and about ten round tables could be placed strategically to house the wedding reception activities. Level 3 was bifurcated and lived on both sides of the barn equally and housed four to five round tables for a sit-down dinner.

The owners took great pride in finding antique gems and loved sharing their new accessories with their friends and guests. Too numerous to mention, the barn was complete with a weather vane, saw blade, bathtub (which we filled with Wisconsin beer), saddles, ropes, pulleys, and levers that made the place a living breathing museum of farm treasures.

The owners were wonderful from day one, and they embraced the fact that their barn was going to be the host site of a wedding between two women, and they were enthusiastically determined to make it the very best it could possibly be for the two brides.

Over the course of the time leading up to our big day, the owners were warm, helpful, and always accommodating to our wishes, and the vendors that would be of service for the affair. We consider ourselves truly blessed that our hosts decided to share their magical farm with the Kirrs and Simpsons.

It's absolutely amazing all the decisions that you have to make when hosting a wedding in a facility that is not a full-time catering hall. Even though the barn is used by friends and relatives a few times a year for weddings and parties alike, you are forced to think of every single detail that needs attention.

The setting forced us to coordinate the rental and/or purchase of tables, chairs, linens, silverware, stemware, and glasses, flowers, centerpieces, bathroom hand towels, napkins, tents, and fans. Looking back, I am absolutely amazed by the amount of planning that would go into making the affair a success.

A year and a half sounds like plenty of time to plan a wedding. In retrospect, we could have used a few more months. However, when the day arrived, we were somehow ready, and it was all systems go.

The day began at our house with Jordy and her bridesmaids all having their hair and makeup done beautifully by local professionals. Unbeknown to me, this four hour ritual is accompanied by a smorgasbord, an open bar, and dance music that reverberated throughout the entire house, setting the tone for the day ahead.

On the other side of town, Jaclyn, her bridesmaids, and her man of honor along with accompanying boyfriends were also enjoying great food, drink, and tunes, putting the entire bridal party in the mood for a day of celebration.

Jaclyn had procured a beautiful and cavernous home on Airbnb for her entire bridal party to enjoy, and that's exactly what they did.

My day was filled with making sure that everyone had everything they needed to get prepared for the big event. I was also charged with making sure that the grandparents were dressed and ready to go for pictures, which would begin several hours before the 6:00 p.m. ceremony.

At around 3:00 p.m., a gleaming massive black coach pulled into our driveway at the appointed time. It was beautiful and was more than spacious enough for Jordy, parents, grandparents, brother, and all of Jordy's bridesmaids.

What a sight. As the bright sun beat down on the midafternoon concrete, we boarded our coach to take us to the farm. It was, as the Bugs Bunny overture, proclaimed, *"This is it, the night of nights, no more rehearsing and nursing a part, we know every part by heart."* It was showtime.

All the bridesmaids were beautiful, mother and grandmother were radiant, and we men were handsome. Jordy was breathtaking, her dress was elegant, her makeup flawless, and she looked like a porcelain doll.

My heart fluttered when I saw Jordy in her dress. Since she was a little girl, I dreamed of this day when she would take a life partner for better or worse, for richer or poorer, until time. Today would be this day.

Truth be told, I never envisioned Jordy would take another woman to be her spouse. However, I can honestly say that I could not have been happier with whom she chose to go through life. Jaclyn is everything that I would want for my daughter and her happiness. She loves Jordy, she is kind, she is caring, and she will always treat her with respect.

As a father, I only wished for Jordy to find love and happiness in this world, and she found that in Jaclyn.

The drive to the farm took around thirty minutes, a touch longer than in a car as we used a coach-bus-friendly route versus the single-lane back roads that cut through the woods. No worries, we had plenty of time, and we were all enjoying the music and the moment.

Jordy's bridesmaids were all beautiful, intelligent, and fun loving. They attempted to make the trip playful and whimsical in an effort to balance Jordy's nervousness and apprehension. This was really happening; this was Jordy's wedding day!

As we pulled into the main entrance of the farm, the coach driver was directed to stop. I was instructed to exit the coach in order to attach a sign and an array of balloons to a decorative post that was part of the main entrance that would visibly provide an easy landmark for our attending guests.

After performing my duties, I boarded the coach for our grand arrival on the scene. As we meandered down the tree-lined single-lane road that snaked through the property, I felt as if I had just entered the world of the Great Gatsby.

To our immediate left as we entered the grounds was the main residence, a storybook mansion, perfect in every detail. Moving past the main house and further down on the left was a magnificent stable appropriately adorned for the day. The stable would serve as our backdrop for the ceremony while perfectly aligned rows of white wooden folding chairs glistened in the summer sun awaiting our guests.

Last but not least the barn came into view; it sat across from the stable, on the right-hand side of the road and next to a large pasture. It was even more enticing than I ever imagined it would be. Adorned with flowers and lights, the barn radiated a rural sophistication that was magnificent.

Upon our arrival, we were informed that Jaclyn, her brides-maids, and her man of honor were delayed but would be departing their compound within a few minutes, which would still put them at least twenty minutes away. In the meantime, we would focus on taking photos of Jordy with her bridesmaids and our family.

On cue, my wife located the event planner to point out some last-minute details she wanted to button up before our guests started to arrive. The entire scene was amazing. The catering company had brought in extra servers who were scurrying to and fro, put-ting last-minute touches on the beautiful tables. The florist flittered about, making each area more beautiful than it already was, and the band was setting up inside the barn preparing the setting for an eve-ning of lifelong memories.

Two black Lincoln limos finally arrived at the farm and, as Jaclyn and her bridal party exited the vehicles, they were noticeably disturbed as the air-conditioning inside did not work very well. The combination of being uncomfortable and late put a brief damper on the event, but Jaclyn's bridal party pushed through the discomfort, and in short order, they were engaged in their photo session.

The girls had decided that they did not wish to see each other until later in the photo shoot,

When the time arrived, the long tree-lined entrance way made for the perfect setting for the two to meet, as the two beautiful brides saw and gently embraced each other for the first time on their wed-ding day.

As the ladies completed their photos, the guests started to arrive. We were instructed at this time to go behind the stable and wait for the ceremony to begin.

As we attempted to gather the bridal party, the guests were excitedly directed toward an open reception station that was set up on the side of the stable providing our guests with a specialty cocktail or a choice of cold drinks.

We were very fortunate: the weather was almost perfect with bright sunshine, a mild breeze, and temperatures in the low eighties.

Our decision not to tent the lower patio area for the cocktail hour and the upstairs patio off of the main barn entrance provided our guests with an uninhibited breeze and views of the bucolic pasture and the bright blue sky.

Once all of our guests were seated, it was time for the ceremony to take place. A trio provided the music for the ceremony, and from behind the stable, the bridal parties were split up so that Jordy's bridesmaids entered the front of the stable from one side and Jaclyn's from the other.

The bridesmaids proceeded first, followed by the men of honor, and then finally Jaclyn and Jordyn escorted by Jaclyn's mom, Cheryl, Lori, and myself.

The ladies found a wonderful nondenominational officiate to perform the ceremony, and she was perfect. Jordy and Jaclyn chose the content and wrote the vows. The officiate was extremely soulful in her delivery, and her cadence and tone provided for a very sensitive, caring, and loving experience.

Cousin Susan from New York performed a masterful reading, and the ceremony was artfully completed in twenty minutes. I was moved to tears on multiple occasions during the ceremony and during the exchange of vows.

This was the spiritual union of two enlightened and loving souls, and all those in attendance can attest to its beauty.

As the ceremony ended, the party was just beginning, as it was time to celebrate our two brides! The path from the ceremony to the cocktail hour took our guest about two minutes to traverse, as they made their way down a slope and to the lower patio area, furnished with high-top tables and plenty of room to mix and mingle as instrumental music provided a pleasant background for conversation to occur.

Almost immediately, hors d'oeuvres were passed, bars were opened, and everyone wanted to congratulate the two brides on their newly minted marriage. I floated from person to person, table to table to table, and enjoyed the first of ten bottles of water that I would consume on the evening. Lori and I separated during the cocktail hour as we both wanted to visit with as many folks as possible in a very short period of time.

It provided me great pleasure to see the owners of the estate join our party and fit right into our celebration. I would find it hard to believe that anyone that attended this affair could come away with anything less than a sense that love and joy were present.

This affair was no more strained, strange, awkward, or different than any other straight celebration. Those present would go on to comment that the entire ceremony and reception was filled with love.

The hour went quickly, and we all made our way to the main floor, to begin our evening of toasts, dancing, dining, and celebrating.

Amaretto greeted our guests with lively dance music as everyone feverishly set about searching for their table to settle in for the evening. After a few songs, it was time for speeches in honor of the special couple.

The Father 4 the Bridez
My Speech

Staring out over Lake Michigan, from the warmth of her one-room apartment high up in the Wisconsin sky, Jordy smiled. She knew that this day was special, that Jackie was special, and the kiss at Lambeau would live in her heart and mind forever.

In words of that famous golf announcer Jim Nantz, Welcome, friends!

It gives Lori and I great joy to welcome everyone here tonight as we celebrate the love between two wonderful young ladies, Jordy and Jackie.

We would like to begin by acknowledging Jackie's mother, Cheryl, and her grandmother Betty.

It also gives us great pleasure to welcome Jordy's G-Ma, Dolores, and her poppy, Bill.

Our joy would not be complete without Jackie's longtime friend and mentor, Bond Shamansky, and Jordy's older brother, Adam.

We also want to thank all the aunts, uncles, cousins, friends, classmates, teammates, and cell mates, just kidding, wanted to see if you were paying attention, who made the effort to share this special evening with us as well. Please give yourself a big round of applause.

Along the journey to this evening, much has happened and many questions were posed. The one that seemed to somehow always get asked was, "What's the wedding going to be like since it is nontraditional?

My answer has always been the same. What is nontraditional about celebrating the love of two beautiful female souls? Oh, yeah, they both happen to be highly educated, world-class athletes and coaches, loving daughters, granddaughters, cousin, sister, and friend possessing a zeal for excellence and life.

Tonight I have crafted a poem for my two wonderful ladies that I would now like to share with you entitled:

Two to One

2 magnificent points of light from galaxies afar, descended down to earthly plane in search of their soulful star.

Decades passed as time marched on as neither knew the other, they played and danced and grew to be magical worldly wonders.

Until one day their 2 stars aligned and they joined together as 1, for now they knew that 221 is a gift to be cherished for time.

So raise a glass for J and J. May they enjoy a lifetime of health, happiness, prosperity, and a never-ending love for each other! Hear, hear!

The speeches would continue for almost another forty-five minutes as Cheryl, select bridesmaids, and the men of honor would all pay homage to the newlyweds in their own unique and entertaining manner.

The balance of the evening was almost purely a dance marathon, with everyone on the floor enjoying the great sounds of the band from Washington, DC. As the evening progressed, the temperature dissipated, giving way to a very comfortable and star-studded evening sky. It was magical.

I recall walking outside of the barn near the end of the affair and turning back to watch the festivities feeling as if I were part of a dream. The lights from inside of the barn were absolutely stunning against the deep sapphire sky, the music rhythmically suffused the night air, and the brides danced with complete joy surrounded by loving family and friends.

I realized at that moment that I had made the transcendence from embarrassment to embracement, from darkness to light, from ignorance to enlightenment connected to source.

Bowing my head, I thanked God for granting us such a magnificent day, for my beautiful and loving wife, Lori, my son Adam, for our new family members, and of course for Jordy and Jaclyn and how their love provided me the opportunity to find the very best inside of myself.

The End

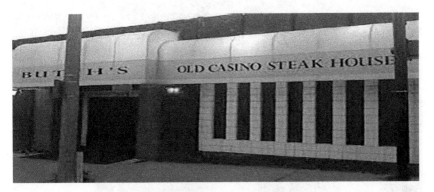

Butch's Restaurant , Milwaukee, WI.

Dinner at Butch's, in the presence of love.

Steve, Jaclyn, and Lori enjoy a postgame victory hug!

Jordy and Jaclyn, engagement toast

Wedmore Inn

Jaclyn, Jordy, Lori, and Steve

A gentle loving embrace

Exchanging Vows

Mrs. & Mrs.

Father 4 the bridez

About the Author

Stephen Kirr was raised in the 1960s and '70s by his steelworker father and stay-at-home mother in the shadows of Bethlehem Steel corporation in Sparrows Point, Maryland.

Steve is the product of twelve years of Christian education, eight at Saint Rita elementary and middle school in old Dundalk, Maryland, and Archbishop Curley High School in Baltimore City.

Upon his 1983 graduation from the University of Maryland, College Park, Steve married his college sweetheart Lori and embarked on raising a family, a son, Adam, now thirty-one, and daughter, Jordyn, twenty-nine, while developing a successful business career that has spanned over three decades.

Along the way, Steve studied the ancient and modern-day gurus and sages dedicating himself to a lifetime of personal growth and spiritual development.

CPSIA information can be obtained
at www.ICGtesting.com
Printed in the USA
BVHW08s2241180918
527890BV00002B/11/P

9 781640 035751